Modern Day
MAGIC

ILLUSTRATIONS BY
CODY BOND

Modern Day
MAGIC

RACHEL LANG

Hardie Grant

BOOKS

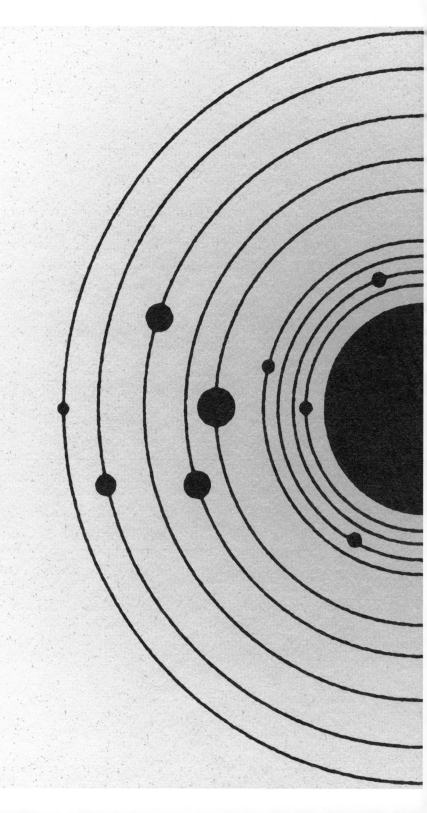

Contents

M
A
G I
C

If you have picked up this book, you are ready for your initiation.

Wonder and curiosity will be your guides;
follow them.

Synchronicity is your messenger,
and you will learn to read its clues.

Awe and gratitude will be your reward,
although you might also manifest some
of your deepest desires.

Together, we are starting on a journey
to discover the hidden magical powers
you lost many lifetimes ago.
You are ready to reclaim them now.
You are ready to live a magical life.

And so it is.

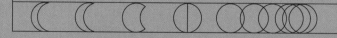

Introduction

Have you ever felt something is missing? Or like you have all of this untapped potential and don't know what that means? Were you sure you were destined for something great, only to find you feel disappointed and frustrated with your life? And even if you've achieved a worldly success, do you crave something more? Do you feel regret and even resentment sometimes? Maybe you feel stuck and ready for a change but lack the passion or courage to make a move.

If you relate to any of this, you're dealing with what I call a "Magic Crisis." Because when you feel this way for a long time, you can feel disconnected, both from others and the natural world. You might set your intentions but face setbacks in actualizing them. Thoughts of worry, anxiety, and fear may preoccupy your mind. You feel judgmental, and you might even turn against yourself and those you love most dearly. You can't put your finger on precisely what's wrong, but you feel helpless to fix it.

If you've ever experienced a Magic Crisis or if you're in one right now, I have good news: the tools, exercises, and rituals in this book will help you break free from restrictions to have a more synchronistic, soulful, and spiritual experience of life. If you're currently stuck in a Magic Crisis, you really can restore your magical power and it doesn't even take work or effort. In fact, it works best if you're having fun! You'll use your imagination, suspend disbelief, and end up adopting a more relaxed approach to life.

I started writing this book after a Magic Crisis of my own. My wife and I were trying to start a family, and what we thought would be a relatively smooth process turned into a three-year journey of self-discovery, heartbreak, grief, and, finally, consolation. I was approaching it all wrong—with my intellect (and probably my ego, too) and not with my magic. I was trying to figure out solutions, obsessively searching outside of myself for answers, rather than listening to my inner wisdom and allowing the mystery of new life to unfold.

Disconnection from magic is systemic. When you feel an absence of it in one area of your life, everything else feels dull and lifeless too. I needed a change. My wife said something that seemed true at the time, "Good things happen when other good things are happening."

While it was true that life was moving forward and there were happy moments, in the big picture, good things were not happening for us, as evidenced by the fact both of us were in a work lull, moving through a grieving process after the loss of her father, and clearly in an overall life transition.

We had blessings, of course, for which we felt grateful, but at the same time, everything felt sort of flat and void of passion. Plus, we'd faced one setback after another in our attempts to bring a child into our family. Couples can have a joint Magic Crisis, and while one person might still have access to their magical power, if the other doesn't, the two can have a difficult time manifesting together. In the middle of our Magic Crisis, I prayed for guidance. It came in an unlikely package. One day, I walked by the Alexandria II bookstore in Pasadena, California, and felt a nudge from some force outside of myself. I heard, "There's something in here for you." I went in and noticed a notebook with the words, "Think in Magic," on the cover.

Now, I'm very particular about my journals; this one was not my style. But I felt a sparkle of resonance in my chest that I have come to identify with magical experiences, and I bought the book.

The first entry on the first page is dated 12 April 2018:

"I saw this book today and thought, I should start a magic journal! I am not quite sure what will come of this, and to be honest, I don't trust myself to stick with it. Ha!"

Then, as if some supernatural force had overtaken my pen, in capital letters and even a different handwriting, I found myself writing:

"MAGIC RULE #1: TRUST YOURSELF."

And thus, it began—my own deep experience of working with magic.

My Magical Story

I've always lived a magical life. As a child, I had regular mystical experiences including visions, dreams, angel messages, and spirit communication. Coming from a Christian (Roman Catholic) background, I was involved in planning liturgies and helped lead a prayer group. So, I understood the importance and significance of ritual practices. I also knew how to structure a ritual. Then, in my late adolescence, I began to explore and practice witchcraft. Around that time, I took development classes from a spiritualist church in the Midwest and learned divination and mediumship skills. I began to understand the connectedness between my mystical experiences in childhood and those I'd had as a witch. The spiritual energy, I realized, was exactly the same.

I was a practicing witch at a very young age but after several very intense experiences, I became afraid of my power. When I was around 21, I attended a public ritual. The High Priestess selected me to place our collective intentions into a burning cauldron and I was so focused on my task I didn't notice the entire left side of my sweater was on fire. As I looked up, I saw both the flames and the look of shock on the High Priestess's face. As our eyes met, the fire disappeared as if it had never been there in the first place.

During another ritual I performed with a friend, we walked out into a field during the full moon. We sat in a clearing, and I led us through the beginning stages of a ritual. Suddenly, a pack of wild dogs formed a circle around us in the dark. They howled in mysterious unison. At that moment, an owl flew low over our heads and hooted, and as suddenly as they had come, the dogs dispersed. Because I started to fear my witchy power and my magic, and because being a non-Christian had set me at odds with my family, I stopped practicing witchcraft and tried to live what I thought was a "normal" life. But once you've accessed your magical power, you can't just turn it off. It reminds you it's there—within you—and you can't ignore your burning desire to awaken to its potential. I tried to suppress it for several years and grew extremely depressed.

Around the time of my Saturn return (at age 29), I realized I could not live my life by half-measures any longer. I returned to my spiritual practice and began to find like-minded others in what was then the spiritual "underground". I started offering astrology consultations and developed my psychic mediumship skills.

I also became fascinated with magical power from an academic perspective.

Helping You Find Your Magical Powers

As I wrote this book, I immersed myself in the work for weekends at a time, learning more and more about how to access my magical power. I wrote most of the book by hand and in that different handwriting I alluded to at the beginning of the chapter. I wrote as if I were channeling the material. And I had fun—working through all these exercises and then sharing them with my wife, clients and friends.

Throughout the writing process, I felt connected, guided and loved. I was held by divine helpers—my spirit guides. They were present with me, and I expect yours will be with you as you read this book.

Magic is, well, *magic*, and when you start playing with it, your life changes. You begin to experience synchronicity and supernatural phenomena because you become more deeply connected to your world and others in it. You start to think in magic and find meaning in even the smallest encounters.

Modern Day Magic is not a book about witchcraft, though I incorporate ideas, rituals, and spells from my experience as a practicing witch. My experience of magic is unique to my life experiences and my hope is that this book will help activate your own unique brand of magical power too. In this book, I've included rituals, daily practices, spells, and writing prompts, each of which have been tried, tested, and refined for you. I designed each one to help you become more comfortable with your power so you that you can access more of it in your life. And just like magic itself, these exercises nudge you to participate and play.

The journal prompts are designed for deeper self-inquiry. They can help you raise subconscious truth into the light of awareness and overcome fears in the process. The magical exercises help you expand spiritual awareness or fine-tune your intuition. In doing so, you can experience more of your magical power. Finally, the spells and rituals offer practical ways to use magic in your everyday life.

Some exercises may just not resonate with you or you may feel too tired to give them your all. That's okay! Gently skip over those and continue with the reading. One of the aims of this book is to help you reclaim and experience your power. Therefore, you have choices.

Together, we will move into some deep waters, and then we will pull out of the depths, lighten up and have a good laugh, do a ritual, and then dive back into the deep end.

I invite you to keep an open mind as you read this book. Let your ego take a break during the meditations. Reserve judgment, suspend disbelief, and trust the process. This book wants your participation, your playful spirit, and, most importantly, your willingness to change. It wants you to tap into the deep well of magical mojo within you, without fear or restraint.

Magic is nonlinear, and so while this book has structure, you may skip from one chapter to another out of sequence. You could also focus on one chapter a week as a thirteen-week program. Each chapter starts with a Daily Practice if you choose to work with the material in this way. In the first chapters, we define magic and offer some basic guidelines for working with this innate power. In Chapters 4–11, I lead you through the "magic rules," which, together, give you everything you need for a magical process.

 ## 8 SIMPLE RULES

#1   ***Trust Yourself—All of Yourself***
#2   ***Magic Is Power***
#3   ***Attention Is Power***
#4   ***Embrace Your Dark Side***
#5   ***Be Whole***
#6   ***Relax and Allow***
#7   ***Ritualize It***
#8   ***Use Magical Astrology***

In the final two chapters, I explore and suggest the different ways you can use your magic in your everyday life to shape your experiences and change your world for the better.

Magic is not about getting something you want (as you'll find out soon in Chapter 2); it's about embodying your prime creative potential. That said, in this book, you will work with a primary intention, a desire you'd like to materialize in your life. By focusing on that one thing, you can hone your magical abilities and become more aware of your own magical power in action. The outcome of your intention doesn't matter for our purposes. What matters more is that you're awakening a dormant energy, becoming more embodied in your power, and learning to focus your attention (which is a form of power) on a specific aim. In fulfilling these goals, you're on your way to living a more magical life.

This is an interactive book, so listen to both your cravings and resistances. I'd encourage you to keep a Magic Journal to record the many magical happenings in your life as you access, test, and explore your own magical powers.

Magic has been a primary theme in my life, and I am so honored to share it with you. Together, we can spread more of it into the giant field of potentiality that surrounds us all—this collective unconscious of ours. And in doing so, we really can work together to create a different kind of world.

A Prayer
for You

I offer you abundant blessings and big love as you read these pages and complete these exercises.

I am right here, cheering you on! I am right here at the threshold, inviting you into the magical realm.

I am right here waving my magic wand, helping you push through fear, resistance, and doubt to open the flow of magical energy in your life.

Now, you are ready. Let's begin.

And so, it is.

Why Magic? Why Now?

1

Welcome. When you picked up this book, you accepted an invitation to embark on an adventure in self-exploration. By opening this page, you've accepted a sacred call to show up in your life in a more powerful way. You see, you're a brilliant creator, with magic coursing through you, but this power has been suppressed. Today, by answering this call, you're crossing a threshold of fear and entering the magical realms, where you can live in everyday awe. This chapter is your first step.

Daily Practice

Gather images of Goddesses or individuals who embody Goddess energy.

Remember, anyone, regardless of gender or sex, can embody Goddess energy.

Anything in nature can, too. Create a digital or paper collage using these images.

Why Magic Got Such A Bad Rap

When you reclaim your magical power, you begin to participate in an unfolding story of creation. No longer will you judge good from bad or right from wrong. Instead, you'll begin to approach all your experiences with curiosity. You'll discover ways to relate with all of creation—the trees, fire, earth, wind, water, and sky. You'll desire knowledge of plants and herbs, attuning yourself to their unique healing properties. You'll become fascinated by the symbolism in all living things and in the stories of the night sky.

A magical life is led by inexplicable and miraculous connections and intertwining storylines. Does this sound intriguing? Then, in order to reclaim your magical power now, we need to go back several centuries and lifetimes to when you had to hide it.

The word "magic" dates back to the 5th century BCE, and it has since been one of the most marginalized and trivialized spiritual concepts of all. The first uses of the word "magic" by the ancient Greeks reflected both an intrigue, and misunderstanding of the religious beliefs and practices of the Persians. It was a derogatory term that the Romans later adopted to use against the Jews. The ancient Jews, however, were also suspicious of magic and sorcery. Jews and Pagans both considered Jesus a magician and used magic as a derogatory term to describe the practices of the early Christians.

The Christians, in turn, used the same rhetoric against the Pagans and went on to condemn witchcraft and associated practices.

So, as you can see, magic has gotten a pretty bad rap. For early patriarchal cultures, differentiating themselves from one another was important because they were drawing borders and establishing jurisdictions. They were colonizing lands, too. Since religion and government went hand in hand, they used a moral basis for their ethnocentrism.

Church and state officials led propaganda campaigns to instill fear of magic and witchcraft. Epic chronicles extolled the horrors of witchcraft. Woodcut fliers depicted horrifying scenes of demons and witches to engender a widespread fear of witchcraft and supernatural power. Witchcraft was a crime punishable by execution, and its targets were mostly women. Colonization led settlers to use similar tactics against indigenous people living in the Americas, Africa, Australia, and New Zealand.

We were set against one another, tortured, and burned alive. We hid, growing fearful of our healing power. Language, tradition, and rites were passed down in secret, if at all. Many of these were simply lost.

Our collective mind holds these memories and feels this trauma. We have these fears and beliefs embedded in our unconscious. While magic has become more popular and witchcraft more widely accepted in recent times, we still have those ancient layers of fear lying between ourselves and our magical powers.

To access your magical powers, you have to remove those layers of fear.

You might not feel you have unfettered access to your own power and purpose, but you do! Your ego has simply shielded you from accessing it because it was afraid that you'd fall out of line, suffer from other people's unkind or cruel judgments, or get into trouble some other way. You've come to fear your sacred, supernatural power. Your light. But your soul longs for you to liberate yourself from this fear.

I see magic as the unifying spiritual force we need right now. It's been at the margins, along with those who have been its guardians, but in it lies our hope for changing the imbalances of power in our relationships, families, communities, businesses, and governments. We live in an exciting and transformational time. We stand on the precipice of a paradigm shift. And while we still have a long way to go, patriarchal and hierarchical structures have started to collapse.

Like the Fall of Rome, these structures will leave behind ruins. In our present-day context, these will be in the form of outdated laws, buildings, ideas, statues, religious icons, and maybe even economic systems. We will bear witness to this time of transition as we restore balance, drawing from the wisdom of our indigenous ancestors as we mold and shape a new earth.

We will be the record-keepers, those of us who watch it all happen. You are one of those people, and the more you access your magical power, the more you participate in the recreation of our new earth.

It is that simple and that profound.

The Goddess

One of the ways we can liberate ourselves from past spiritual beliefs and ideas is to welcome an experience of the Divine Feminine—the Goddess.

The spiritual concept of the Divine Feminine has been with us for centuries. She moves through us in innumerable ways, regardless of our gender and sex. She's the life-giving fertility goddess Diana, the grieving mother Demeter, the compassionate mother Quan Yin, the beautiful love-goddess Aphrodite, the warrior craftswoman Athena, the queen mother Hera, and the heroine of discord, Eris. She's the Holy Spirit and Mother Mary. Sophia wisdom. Inanna, Lakshmi, Persephone, Kali, Eve, Lilith, and Esther. She's Shakti and Gaia. She's you.

While I refer to specific goddesses and representations of the Divine Feminine, we don't want to limit Her to any one of these images or icons. The Divine Feminine, the Goddess, is the presence of the Divine that's alive and palpable in our world—in nature, humans, and even the stars. She's the connecting force between energy and matter. When you invoke the Goddess, you feel Her as a spiritual force moving through your body as the Power of Presence.

Magical processes involve activity and receptivity. They involve (1) intention-setting, (2) focusing our power, and (3) action steps. Then, after we've done all we can, we wait, feel, and receive. We allow the process to unfold, feeling the different steps we need to take or those aspects of ourselves we need to heal through the guidance of our intuition. The Goddess wants our quietude, and the more impatient we feel and the more we wonder what we can *do*, the more She gently nudges us to wait. She teaches us to let go and trust. She carries our intentions to us through the forces of the wind, water, earth, fire, and spirit. She delivers guidance through other people or elements of nature.

When I think of the Divine Feminine, I picture Sandro Botticelli's painting *Nascita di Venere*—The Birth of Venus in which the innocent, nubile Venus stands nude on a half-shell in the sea. The wind god Zephyr blows her to shore, where the Hora of Spring awaits her arrival with open arms. Venus isn't paddling her way through the sea foam. Nor is she asking Zephyr, "Are we there yet? What can I do to speed this up?" Venus remains relaxed and at ease. She allows the spirit to carry her to her intended destination.

Receptivity is powerful. Next time you wonder, "What should I *do* to manifest my intention," think of Venus. Place your hand over your heart and embody the Goddess. Then, ask instead, "How should I *be* for my intention to come to me with grace and ease?"

Spirit time moves in an elegant rhythm. Sometimes, it inches along, and at other times, it moves at lightning speed. Things like intuitive impressions, messages conveyed in divination, and spiritual guidance arise into conscious awareness. You have to be still to receive, and sometimes, it can feel impossibly slow. So, too, do your intentions manifest in spirit time, often when you least expect them or when you're busy looking the other way.

When you let go of control and release your intention into the heart of the Divine, the Divine Feminine enlivens the elements. The winds blow you to your destination. The earth sends signals to helpful people who unexpectedly appear in your life to guide your way. Magic flows right to you.

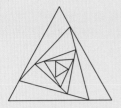

MAGICAL EXERCISE:

Invoking the Goddess

1. Either lie on the ground with your arms wide open or on a bed surrounded by soft, plush pillows. I prefer to do this exercise outside and facing the ground, so I'm hugging the earth.

2. Close your eyes. Set an intention to breathe the Goddess into your body with every breath. Feel your face resting against the earth (or your pillow). Experience Her as a divine mother holding you.

3. Does a picture come to mind? An image of her as Mother Mary, Quan Yin, Artemis, Isis, a dove, or something else?

4. Feel or imagine the earth's subtle rocking as she rotates on her axis and slowly revolves around the sun. Ask the Goddess to heal any conflicts you have with your mother. Feel Her presence throughout your body.

Journal Prompt

WRITE A LETTER TO THE GODDESS STATING YOUR PRIMARY INTENTION. INVOKE HER (SEE PAGE 23) AND THEN WRITE A LETTER BACK TO YOURSELF AS IF SHE'S WRITING TO YOU. DON'T WORRY IF THE WORDS YOU WRITE SEEM AS IF THEY ARE COMING FROM YOUR IMAGINATION AND NOT HER. IF YOU CAN'T QUITE FEEL HER, IT'S OKAY. TAKE YOUR TIME. ALLOW THE WORDS TO FLOW IN A STREAM OF CONSCIOUSNESS TO OPEN YOUR CHANNELS OF CREATIVITY.

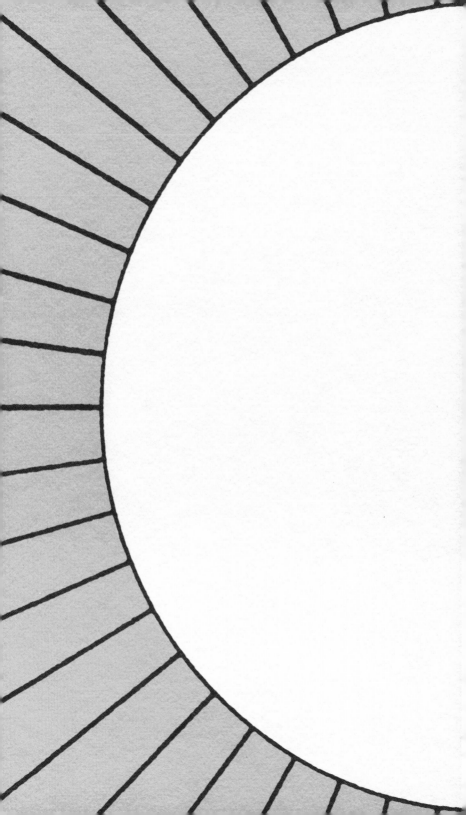

The Time to Reclaim Your Power Is Now

We have a long way to go to purify and heal our collective psyches. But we're so intimately and intricately connected that when you heal yourself and begin accessing your magical power, you help change the consciousness of the whole world too.

Some of you may already embrace your witchy side. Maybe you've been a practicing witch for years but as with any implicit bias, you will need to eradicate those subconscious, collective ideas and fears about witchcraft if you are to claim and access your magical powers. It's crucial. You cannot fully access your power and fear it at the same time.

So, for a moment, close your eyes and visualize a witch. What do you see? What feelings do you have as you imagine this person? Think of your own power. Journal your thoughts and sign and date the entry.

Magic is a deeply embodied experience. Magic isn't transcending up into the sky to connect with the Divine; it's opening your heart, grounding yourself in nature, and being the Divine here on earth. Magic, then, doesn't become simply about manifesting what you want; it becomes a way of life that seeks participation with all.

You are ready to take the next steps on your journey to reclaiming and working with your magical power. The writing exercise opposite can help you reach back through time and reconnect with your power.

Journal Prompt

WHEN WAS THE FIRST TIME YOU FELT YOUR MAGICAL POWER?

WHAT EXPERIENCES IN YOUR LIFE CAUSED YOU TO FEAR YOUR POWER?

IN RECLAIMING YOUR MAGICAL POWER, HOW WILL YOUR LIFE CHANGE?

What Is Magic?

2

In this chapter, you'll restructure your notions of what magic is and is not. We will deconstruct any preconceived ideas about magic. Then, you will define it for yourself.

Daily Practice

Each morning, ask yourself "What is one thing I can do to feel more joy today?"

Prioritize that one thing and make time to enjoy life.

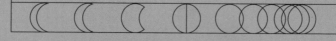

Magic: Working With Supernatural Power

Magic is the creative spiritual energy that courses through your body, enlivens every cell, and connects you with every atom in the universe. It bends, shifts, and transforms energy. It makes something out of nothing. It links two people in different parts of the world, stimulating synchronistic events so that, although they are thousands of miles apart, they feel a similar resonance. It is a "sparkle" in your chest, an effervescence you feel in your body. Its gentle force can make you smile with delight, laugh, cry tears of gratitude, or burn with passion or fury deep inside the pit of your stomach. Magic is passion enlivened. It is creative, life-giving, and deeply feeling. It awakens life inside you.

You will experience magic differently to anyone else in the world because your magic is unique to you. I will share ideas about what I've come to discover about magic. And like magic, your own description will evolve. After all, magic isn't only an intellectual concept; it's a palpable, sensual flow of creative and spiritual energy.

If you look up the word "magic" in the dictionary, you will likely see something like this:

NOUN

The power of apparently influencing events by using mysterious or supernatural forces.

ADJECTIVE

1. Having or apparently having supernatural powers.
2. Wonderful; exciting.

VERB

Move, change, or create by or as if by magic.

The general explanation involves the use of supernatural powers to manifest some change. I like the definition offered by Starhawk, author of a book called *The Spiral Dance: Rebirth of the Ancient Religion of the Goddess*: "The art of changing consciousness at will." In magic, we can intend to change our individual consciousness, but all life has consciousness, and we share a collective consciousness as well. So, magic is a power from within that affects change not only in your life, but also in your community and the world as well.

Sounds pretty incredible, right? Well, as we saw in our brief history lesson in Chapter 1, "magic" has always been the religious "other." If you grew up with religious bias about witchcraft and magic, or if you disbelieve in magic, you may now want to start shifting your consciousness so that you can access all of your inherent power.

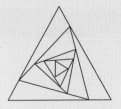

Rejecting Preconceived Ideas

1. Set a timer for two minutes. Open your Magic Journal and write: *What I Used to Think of Magic.* Start the timer and write a list of whatever comes to you in a stream of consciousness.

2. Now, take a deep breath. On a separate blank piece of paper, write: *What I Want to Feel Right Now.* Set a timer for two minutes. Write in a stream of consciousness every word or idea that comes to mind.

3. Light a white or black candle. On your page marked *What I Used to Think of Magic* you will create an art piece over the words with paint, collage, marker, crayon, or any other supplies. Start by covering all the words until you can't see any text. As you do, say: *I release all preconceived ideas I have about magic. I start today with a clean slate and allow myself to explore and define what magic means for me. I am willing to experience the fullness of my power.*

4. On the page titled *What I Want to Feel Right Now* paint, draw, or collage over the clean slate you've just created. As you do, feel all of those feelings. Allow yourself to give in to the experience.

5. Magic is part left brain and part right. Art helps you access both sides. End the exercise by snuffing the candle and saying, *And so it is. Blessed be.*

My Magic—Your Magic

Magic is not just about manifesting a desire, although manifestation can happen as a result of magic. When you think in magic, you see the world through the eyes of a child—with awe and wonder. You can sense the world in terms of energy and frequency. When a hawk flies overhead, you ask, "What is the symbolism of this? What is this hawk trying to say to me?" When you see repeating number sequences, you understand there are energetic forces of synchronicity at play. When we work with magic, the boundaries and separateness between ourselves and the natural world seem to disappear.

My exploration of magic started when I discovered the New Age section of the public library. At the time, my parents were a part of the Catholic Charismatic movement—an unofficial group of Holy Spirit Catholics. Growing up, I learned to access my spiritual gifts within this religious foundation. I spoke in tongues, participated in healing services, received prophetic messages, talked with angels, had visions, and felt the power of the Holy Spirit.

In adolescence, I became fascinated with spirituality and religion. I loved the mystical tradition of the Catholic Church, the ritual practices of the sacraments, and the teachings of Jesus that were centered around love and mercy. Yet, as a fledgling feminist, I sought a more open and inclusive spiritual experience. I explored witchcraft, Buddhist meditation, and Spiritualism. I wanted to be my witchy, New Age, Buddhist, mystical self without totally abandoning my Christian foundation. What I sought was uncategorizable—it was magic.

Maybe you're looking for the same thing: to live your experience of spirituality without a narrow definition. Perhaps you want to pray to God *and* put your crystals out at the full moon in order to cleanse them (see Touchstones, page 56). Or maybe you're ready to make a transition from the religious practices of your childhood to ones more relevant to this current phase of your life.

The good news is you don't have to be an initiated witch to be magical or to access your magical powers. Magic is not a religion; it's a way of life. You can incorporate magic into any spiritual belief system.

Magic Is Ecstatic!

Magic is our spiritual essence, unedited and whole. It binds us together, and when we experience it, we experience a mystical oneness—that feeling you have when you're in complete synchrony and in awe over the signs and symbols you see in both your dreams and your waking life.

The spiritual energy we're talking about is sensed and felt through the body. It's a force within you that stimulates desire. Desire motivates the will to change. It spurs you on to reach beyond your comfort zone, to take a risk, fall in love, have a baby, write a book, start a new job, or change your life in some way.

Magic stems from an intuitive and emotional place within the self, far from the conscious mind and deep within our hearts and bodies. It's also tied to our passions. The fear of magic has been a fear of this power, of sexuality, and of the body throughout time. Primarily, it's a fear of the feminine.

Remember a time when you fell in love. In the beginning stages of a relationship, your pleasure centers heighten, and you feel everything at maximum capacity. You feel as if anything is possible, even if slight relationship-related fears crop up from time to time. Love at a great magnitude cancels out fear, which can block the flow of magic in your life.

When you have a crush on someone, it's a similar vibe. In those times of heightened energy and attraction, you may feel more creative or motivated to make changes in your life. You might learn to play an instrument that you know they like, change your style, work out, or write poetry for the first time. The outcome of the relationship doesn't matter to your magical self; the sensations and feelings do.

When my clients come to me with questions about a budding relationship or a crush, I often encourage them to go with it! To feel all the feelings to the *nth* degree without worry or fear of ruining the experience. Of course, I always advise them to maintain their integrity and keep healthy boundaries, as we can still feel that energy without ever acting it out sexually.

Magic flows unrestricted through ecstasy. In many ritual practices, participants are brought to altered states of consciousness through drumming, dancing, chanting, swaying, swirling, singing, or even sex. In this state of consciousness, you feel a heightened sense of peace, joy, love, and sometimes, bliss.

Ecstasy tempers the mind, allowing you to feel "at-oneness." In this state, you become more receptive to the energies around you and can intuitively send and receive signals. In this state, your nonlinear right brain becomes activated, and you feel less fear, judgment, or doubt, which can otherwise restrict the flow of magical energy.

But ecstasy doesn't always feel good. Sometimes, you can achieve an altered state when you feel a sudden and overwhelming surge of intense emotion, including grief, despair, or sorrow. The kind of feeling you have, for example, right after the loss of a loved one, an accident, or the diagnosis of an illness. Times of grief can also be times when your magical power flows freely because the swell of emotion forces you into the present moment, and in doing so, temporarily disengages you from your fearful ego. That said, you don't want to intentionally raise this kind of energy in your body on a day-to-day basis to do your magical work. There are more enjoyable, pleasurable ways to open the flow of magic.

For some of you, the idea of ecstasy may seem intriguing but unattainable, especially if you've been in a Magic Crisis. Some of you might not feel comfortable letting go of your sense of control. Perhaps you've never experienced being in an altered state of consciousness, nor can you relate to being overcome by intense emotion. Maybe you've always lived on an even keel, comfortable with a specific but more limited range of emotions. Opening yourself to magic is opening yourself to a richer panoply of emotions and experiences. Let's try it together.

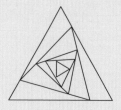

MAGICAL EXERCISE:

Experiencing Ecstasy

1. Repeat this mantra three times: *I am willing to release all inhibitions, allowing myself to be a vessel for spiritual, magical energy. Let it course through my veins. Let it flow through me, filling spaces where fear used to dwell.*

2. Think of one of your happiest memories, one that makes you feel giddy. No judgment here! Just go with the first thing that comes to your mind, even if it's not what you might consider a "spiritual" moment.

3. Once you've settled on a memory, allow a smile to spread across your face and in your heart. Feel that smile throughout your body, from head to toe. Take your time with this and allow the happy feeling to move through you.

4. If you notice any tight areas of your body or any places where the blissful feeling won't flow through, then move your body in whatever ways it wants, and allow that energy in. For example, if your shoulders feel tight, roll them backward and forward. If you have injuries or health issues in any area of your body, spend a little extra time there. If you're doing this right, you should be wiggling and swaying and moving like no one's watching. Keep moving until every cell in your body feels lighter, looser, and happier.

5. When you feel the energy moving freely throughout your body, be still. Place your arms at your sides just in front of you so that your palms are facing one another about a foot apart. Focus all of that energy from your body into your hands. Now, move your hands toward one another an inch at a time, but do not allow them to touch. What do you feel? Hold the sensation for a few moments and feel that energy.

6. Now, visualize that energy as a ball of white light with glittery sparkles. Watch it in your imagination grow brighter and brighter. Keep going back to the happy feeling you've had throughout this exercise and send that feeling from your heart into your hands.

7. With a long inhale and exhale, throw that ball of light down to the earth.

8. Shake any excess energy out of your body. Pat your arms, shoulders, and legs to ground yourself. Feel the soles of your feet touch the earth floor as you close the ceremony.

Magic
Rule of Three

As you perform the Experiencing Ecstasy exercise (page 38), you may notice two things:

1. Although you've shared your magical energy with the earth, you probably feel like you have more of it than you did before you sent it down to the ground.

2. You'll likely feel a little lighter and more connected with the sensations in your heart.

Magical energy is in constant flow. You shouldn't feel depleted after working with magic because you're drawing energy from the elements. When you share magic with intention and goodwill, you generate more for yourself.

Magic Rule of Three: The energy you send out into the universe spirals back to you threefold.

Whatever energy you conjure in your magical work, you will likely feel even more of it in all areas of your life. Think of your energy like solar- or wind-powered electricity. It's a renewable resource available whenever you need it. You can plug into it and recharge anytime. When I feel exhausted, I often tap the top of my head (my crown chakra) and say to myself, "I'm downloading more energy."

At the same time, when you want to focus your magical power toward a particular manifestation, keep the Magic Rule of Three in mind. Clear away any frustrations, disappointments, regrets, judgments, or resentments.

Before performing your rituals and spells, take a few deep breaths and release any feelings or thoughts you wouldn't want to return to you threefold. When you're first working with magic and reclaiming your power, it's helpful to clear your energy regularly. A simple way to do this is by taking a long, relaxing salt bath, as salt can neutralize your energy body—which we also call our aura.

Magic
Is Embodied

We perform exercises like Experiencing Ecstasy to have a physical, bodily experience of energy so that we can then begin working with it more intentionally. We will continue to anchor ourselves in the body, as it will be our primary source of guidance as we work with magic.

If you have pain in your body, have experienced trauma, or are self-critical about certain physical features, you might feel disconnected from your body. Fear, pain, and judgment can do that. To be magical, wholly inhabit your body: the cellulite, wrinkles, freckles, sore joints, and all. Love your body and relish all of its pleasurable sensations—good food, physical touch, soft blankets, sex, dance, movement, and more.

Working with magic, we're working with the body and the signals it sends. Emotions are our body's responses to internal and external stimuli. When you are sad, you might feel a twinge of tightness in your heart. Your eyes water slightly, and your mouth turns downward. Your body sends you clues to attune you to your heart.

Your bodily sensations are also intuitive informants. Have you ever felt butterflies in your stomach for no apparent reason, only to have a life-changing experience shortly afterward? When you start working with magic, you begin tuning into these signals and becoming more aware of the messages they are offering you. By tuning in to your body more intentionally, you can better access and trust your intuition.

Body Awareness Exercise

Once you know your inner *yes* and inner *no*, you can answer almost any question you have in your life.

For this exercise, think of your body as one giant pendulum. Stand or sit in a comfortable upright position. Tap lightly on your chest three or four times with the palm of your hand. Cross your hands over the top of your chest.

Relax your body by taking a few deep breaths. Let your body sway gently from side to side, then front to back. Find your center again. Now, state to yourself: *The grass is green.*

See which way your body naturally sways. Most often, when I teach this, the body leans forward for *Yes* and backward for *No.* State to yourself: *The sky is yellow.* Wait for the response. Try other *yes* or *no* statements. *My name is Bob. My name is _____ (state your name). I am magical.*

When you ask a more complicated question, maybe there isn't a clear *yes* or *no* answer. You can break it down until it becomes more apparent. For example, state to yourself: *I am ready to manifest my intention.*

Which way do you lean? If you lean backward, ask another question, like: *After doing the exercises in this book, I will be ready.* Or: *I will be ready when I face my fear.* You can keep asking *yes* or *no* questions until you have a breakthrough.

Think of the phrase, "I'm leaning toward this or that." Your body does this regularly. When someone with whom you don't want to interact approaches you, you might naturally lean away. When you are in an exciting conversation, you might lean in towards the person with whom you're speaking. The more you become aware of your body's natural responses, the more you can rely upon that information for clarity about your life.

Keep practicing this exercise until you have it down to a science. Eventually, you won't need to sway at all. If you continue to develop this awareness, you'll be able to feel the difference between *yes* and *no.*

Basics Before We Begin

3

In this chapter, we will cover a few basics about working with magic. You will set a primary intention—something you'd like to see come to fruition in your life. Having a specific focus for your magical work will help you access your power. You may not ever manifest the exact outcome you'd like, but that's okay. When you work with magic, if something doesn't manifest, then new possibilities arise.

Daily Practice

Set a scheduled time to connect with your divine helper once a day. Use the guided meditation in this chapter (see page 55) to facilitate the connection. What guidance do they have to offer? What messages do you hear? Start building a deeper relationship with your guides.

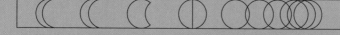

This book is all about the supernatural power you've always had. But like electricity, this power needs to be grounded and directed in specific ways. That's why we start with the basics which are:

1. **Purify Your Intent**
2. **Participation and Co-creation, Not Control**
3. **Protect Yourself, Your Space, and Your Energy**
4. **Your Divine Helper**
5. **Build Your Magical Toolbox**

Purify Your Intent

The magical process involves intention and attention. It starts with intention, whether conscious or unconscious. Conscious intentions are the ones you say aloud or think, such as, "I'd like to start a new career" or "I'm ready to fall in love."

Unconscious intentions are those informed by your emotions, beliefs, wishes, and fears. There are times when we state intentions without even realizing that's what we're doing. Maybe your partner breaks up with you, and you think, "This hurts so much. I will never love like this again." Or you hear a baby crying on an airplane and think, "Having kids seems hard and not for me." When you start to work with magic, you realize that every thought or feeling can be a magical spell.

Stating an intention is a powerful process and one you shouldn't take lightly. After all, you just might manifest that intention! When you declare an intention, ask yourself a few questions:

1. Does my intention compromise the free will of anyone else?
2. Could my intention cause harm to another person, a creature, or anything in nature?
3. Does my intention have any unintended consequences?

Working with magic means being aligned with nature and other people. It doesn't mean dominating them. For example, maybe you *really* want your crush to fall for you. Sure, you could use your magic to try to pull that person's focus towards you but imagine being with someone who doesn't love you freely or who feels they're under a spell. How do you think that relationship would be? Not only is it unethical to usurp someone's free will, but it's also not fun for you!

Instead, open yourself to possibilities. Rather than focus your attention on attracting a specific person, set an intention to attract a romantic partner into your life with whom you can share a healthy, harmonious, and loving relationship. In stating your intention, be clear in your mind about what you want and what constitutes a healthy relationship for you.

Your primary intention might involve a career change. If you have a specific job in mind, great! Hold that thought. It's a template for what you desire, a starting point. Think of the qualities of the new position that appeal to you. Then, set an intention to draw a similar job into your life. It might go something like this:

I intend to work with a cooperative team in a leadership role with opportunities for professional development and career expansion.

Here is a set of simple guidelines for structuring an intention:

A. Feel your intention as you're writing it. Take time with it, and maybe let it ruminate for a few days until it resonates with you.
B. Always state your intention in the present tense, not the future or past.

C. State your intention in the positive, not the negative. For example, rather than focus on getting out of debt, intend to experience more prosperity and abundance.

D. Add to your intention the words, "This or better." That way, you stay open to every possibility.

E. Keep it simple. Stay away from *who, where, why,* and *how.* Focus instead on what you're intending. Allow the universe to handle the rest.

If your body feels tight or tense when you say your intention, try using different words until it clicks. Look back at the primary intention you wrote down at the beginning of this chapter. Are there any changes you'd like to make? Do you need to reword it? Does it still resonate with you? If so, make those adjustments and tune into your heart to make sure it resonates. If you don't have changes to make, write it again in bold letters and own it!

Journal Prompt

THINK ABOUT AN INTENTION ON WHICH YOU'D LIKE TO FOCUS. CLOSE YOUR EYES AND DRAW ALL OF YOUR AWARENESS INTO YOUR HEART. WHAT DESIRE ARISES FROM DEEP INSIDE OF YOU? WHAT WOULD YOU LIKE TO CREATE IN YOUR LIFE OR THE WORLD?

Participation and Co-Creation, Not Control

Working with magic means you open the boundaries between yourself and the world of ideas and possibilities. It means you share your desires with the natural world to support the growth and evolution of others and our planet. When you're rigidly fixed on a specific outcome, you exit the realm of magic and enter the realm of control.

When you begin to work with magic, it's easy to give your intention a timeline: "I want to meet and fall in love with my life partner by March 5." Can you feel the limits of time? What happens if, by March 5, you are still very single? You begin to doubt your magical power. Try this instead, "I intend to meet my life partner in the timing that works for our highest good. I trust it can happen with grace and ease." Divine timing is not human timing. Trust you're in a magical process and allow it to unfold.

The most playful, curious part of you is also the most magical. So, it's important to honor that part of you by being open to outcomes which are not as you envisioned or within your hoped-for timeline.

For example, when I work with clients who want to start a family, I often hear the message, "Your baby spirit wants to be born at a different time." Sometimes, I see the baby spirits coordinating with their future partners, cousins, or friends. And yet, for couples trying to conceive, the wait can be excruciating.

How do you know when you're shifting from participation to control? You'll know when your body tenses up; you feel tight in your shoulders, you're constipated, you want to pout, or you have judgmental thoughts.

Protect Yourself, Your Space, and Your Energy

People often ask, "How do you protect yourself from bad spirits?" The truth is you have a lot of control over what happens in your magical practice. The best way to protect yourself is to continue to improve yourself: live with integrity, love yourself and others, be authentic, and follow the Magic Rules. Then, your light and your power will fill your aura, leaving no space for anything else. Beam goodness out from your heart through your entire body and beyond. See your light shining out into the world.

You have the power to allow or deny any spiritual presence to take over your body and life. You're in charge.

During the times you are most magical, your power is a boundary of protection. Think about an empty cup. You can fill it with just about anything, right? Juice, water, tea, soda, bleach, or lighter fluid! Your body and energy field are similar. When you fill your energy field with your light and power, you leave no space for anything else. Take up your space. Be so big in your life and the world that you leave no room for unwanted forces. When you start activating the magic within you, and as you meditate, pray, or perform a ritual, your auric field expands. When you begin growing your aura, you start to be more attractive to others. Your aura is like one great big magnet, and the bigger your aura, the more magnetic it gets. So, when you're doing the exercises in this book and experimenting with your magical power, you'll start to more easily draw experiences and people into your life that resonate with the magical energy you emanate.

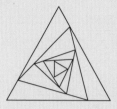

MAGICAL EXERCISE:

See Your Aura

1. Anyone can learn to see auras. Stand in front of the mirror and focus your attention on an invisible point two inches above your head.

2. Let your gaze soften and relax. You will first see an outline of your body in light.

3. Let yourself space out like you're in a daydream or as if you're looking at one of those *Magic Eye* pictures that were so popular in the '90s. Then, you'll start to see colors, shapes, textures. You might even see sparkles or what looks like glitter. You could see cloudy patches; these could be thoughts or emotions.

4. The more you practice, the more you train yourself to "see". It also helps to practice with someone else. So, why not find a magical partner, and play.

Your Divine Helper

A divine helper is a spirit guide (or group of guides) who offers magical assistance, wisdom, and guidance beyond anything you could know without this help. You'll be working closely with your divine helper to build a strong relationship. Over time, they will become your trusted friend and ally in spirit.

MEDITATION:

Calling Your Divine Helper

Visualize a staircase. Walk up five stairs and see yourself in a room with a large conference table. Sit at the table. In front of you, you see a list of names. Notice the names. As you read the names, you will feel "Beings" approach. Who are they?

Maybe they are loved ones who have passed away. Maybe they are friends or family members who are still alive. Perhaps they're a celebrity you admire. Your list may include someone unfamiliar to you. Do not judge the list. Keep an open mind.

Watch these spirits enter the room and sit next to you. Ask one of them if they would like to be your primary divine helper while you learn magic. Relax and allow that spirit to come forward. Feel their love and support.

If the person coming forward is someone in your life and still alive, you could be working with their higher self. (Keep an open mind.) Ask your divine helper if they have any messages to offer you. Sit still and receive.

When you have received the messages you need, thank each one of your divine helpers. Feel their gratitude in return. Then, leaving the list of names on the table, visualize walking back down the steps. Count in your head: 5, 4, 3, 2, 1. When you reach the end of the staircase, wiggle your fingers and your toes, and open your eyes.

Build Your
Magical Toolbox

These items will be yours to invoke and use at any time. Feel free to add more tools than I have listed that resonate with you.

Touchstone

Choose a stone (or crystal) to be your magical touchstone. You will charge this stone to help with grounding your energy and reminding you of your power. Ideally, this stone would be small enough to hold during a ritual or when you're going into a high-pressure situation and need a gentle reminder that you're not alone. Find a stone that resonates with you. When you find your stone, hold it in your palm or focus your gaze on it. Say either aloud or in your mind:

> *Touchstone, I invoke you as one of the tools I will use to become more magical. I charge you as a Protector Stone. I ask you to absorb any energy that negates my magic power, and I allow you to ground my energy so that I can focus it according to my desires.*

Carry your touchstone with you for a week or place it underneath your pillow as you sleep to charge it fully.

When you find or purchase a stone, clear it from past associations by soaking it in salt water for an hour or so, or leave it outside in the light of the full moon. The new moon is excellent for setting intentions and charging a new stone with an assignment. Ask your stones for protection, healing, positive energy, or help in your magical work.

Each stone has specific properties that can assist in your magical efforts. Here are a few of my favorites.

AMETHYST

Supports spiritual attunement, assists with psychic impressions, provides a balance between head and heart, heals emotional upset, enhances compassion, and protects you in magical work.

CELESTITE

Connects to angels and divine helpers, acts as a messenger stone, supports creativity, dispels worries, assists divination, and helps you know your purpose.

CITRINE

Helps clear negative energies, supports self-confidence, attracts abundance, helps resolve financial concerns or fears, inspires creativity, and promotes a sense of wellbeing.

CLEAR QUARTZ

Offers clarity, lifts thoughts and intentions, brings harmony, cleans energy, supports balance and healing, and amplifies energy.

HEMATITE

Grounding and protection, balances chakras, dissolves negative energy, and helps in meditation for clarity.

JASPER

Grounds energy, offers nurturing, calms stress, aligns chakras, facilitates dreamwork, and protects the body.

LABRADORITE

Raises consciousness, clears energy, supports psychic abilities, and dissolves fear.

MOONSTONE

Assists with divination, fertility rituals or spells, helps creative projects, enhances imagination and intuition, protects travelers, assists clairvoyance, and awakens empathy.

OBSIDIAN

Protects, absorbs negative energy, and dissolves stress.

ROSE QUARTZ

Supports unconditional love, opens heart chakra, fosters peace and harmony, balances polarities, helps heal heartbreak, and supports love magic rituals or spells.

When you find a magical object in nature, connect with the land's indigenous people and honor that land's history. Ask the earth for permission to take the item. Feel the response. With any gift the earth offers you, offer something back in return. Go within and ask what you can give in gratitude for the item, whether a prayer, seed, stone, flower, or promise.

If you are buying an object, your money is enough of a give-back, but know where the item came from. Picture the place and say a thank you in your mind.

Altar

An altar is a sacred workspace designated for your rituals and other spiritual work. You can turn any surface into an altar. Sometimes, I use my desk as an altar. I clear any clutter, place different crystals at the corners, and light a candle. Before I start writing, I'll offer a prayer of gratitude, opening my heart and mind to receive divine guidance and wisdom. Everything you do can be a sacred ritual, and therefore, anything and anywhere can be an altar space. That said, I do like to have a designated space, one for meditation or magical practices. It feels grounding, and it helps anchor the energy of the room.

Aura Globe

Visualize a bubble of light all around your body. Think of this as your Aura Globe. When you set dedicated time and space aside to practice, you will want to create a sacred space, one filled with your magical power, your energy. Invoking the Aura Globe will allow you to experience your energy, power, and light without other distractions.

Magic Wand

A magic wand is an essential tool that focuses light and spiritual energy to a specific place. It symbolizes the alchemical element of fire. For this, you can use anything with a point—a stick from your yard, a crystal wand, a paintbrush, or a pencil. I have magic wands for different purposes because I try to make every activity that I undertake in my life a magical act. When I paint, I start with an intention, and then my painting becomes a magical experience.

When I cook dinner, I start with an intention and stir that into the pot. So, I have a set of blessed and charged paintbrushes and even a spoon with inlaid stones as my magic wands.

Cauldron

In ancient times, the cauldron was a place for cooking meals and mixing up remedies. Anything placed in a cauldron changes through an alchemical process. You can use any bowl, pot, or container as a cauldron and use it to mix potions, burn written intentions, make herbal tinctures, burn incense, or cook a ritual meal.

Consecrating Your Magical Tools

Place your magical tool on your altar space. Place four candles around it. Have incense burning. Rub your palms together until they feel warm. Place them over your heart and draw your awareness to your heart center. Imagine light filling your body and expanding out through your aura. Now, light the candles and say:

I invoke this (name the magical tool) to be my companion in my magical, ritual acts.

Allow the smoke from your incense to surround the object and say:

I ask it to be an extension of myself and to help focus and direct my magical power. I charge it with the light of my power and set it apart as sacred. I call my divine helper to work within me and through this magical tool. (Add anything else you'd like to intend here ...) And so, it is.

Hold your magical tool to your heart. With eyes closed, feel light from your heart chakra flowing out to the item. Then, hold it up above you, and imagine light from above flowing down and surrounding it. When you feel complete, set the object on your altar space. Offer gratitude to your divine helpers. Then, extinguish the candles. Your magical item is now charged and ready for action!

Magic Rule #1 :

Trust Yourself— All of Yourself

4

You may think you trust yourself, but do you, really? How many times have you made promises to yourself only to let yourself down? If you've ever committed to something like starting a diet, writing a book, or meditating daily and become distracted or lost interest within a few weeks, then you know the feeling of disappointing yourself.

Why does this happen?

Put simply, different parts of yourself have unique (and sometimes competing) wants and needs. In this chapter, we'll discuss the different aspects of yourself, explore why they might not always agree on what they want, and suggest how you can remedy that inner conflict.

Daily Practice

Spend at least five minutes in nature every day. Observe all five senses. What sensations do you feel? What do you see? Hear? Taste? Touch? Notice the elements and how they move around you. Take deep breaths and ground your energy.

Aspects of the Self and Their Competing Needs

We are multifaceted spiritual beings in human forms—souls with a personality in a body. You cannot ever experience yourself as being independent from that great field of our collective consciousness, so that's part of yourself, too.

Let's think of the self as being made up of four different parts like this:

Divine Self / Higher Self / Ego Self / Subconscious Self

Divine Self

Your Divine Self is your pure consciousness—it's your soul, interdimensional and incomprehensible. It's timeless, too. Imagine a cloud. Within a cloud, there are individual drops of water. The Divine Self is like the cloud, and we are all drops of water. We're part of this same cloud, but each having our own individual experiences.

When you have mystical experiences or are deep in prayer or meditation, you will feel a part of the cloud, metaphorically speaking. During these moments, you sense you are one with everything and will experience your inherently magical and loving Divine Self. Within that big cloud of our divine consciousness, each living thing—minerals, plants, animals, and humans—has its own individual consciousness within the whole. But the Divine Self encompasses all.

Higher Self

I like to think of the Higher Self as your inner mediator; it's wisdom personified. Your Higher Self most closely aligns with your Divine Self to understand its purpose as a member of the whole. The Higher Self holds the soul's intentions—the specific experiences it desires to have throughout your lifetime. Some of these experiences may be pleasurable, even happy, like a marriage or the birth of a child. Others may feel challenging or unpleasant, like the loss of a loved one or a divorce. The Higher Self knows exactly which experiences to lead us through for our soul's growth and evolution. And by that, I mean the growth and evolution of consciousness as a whole.

Ego Self

Your Ego self is your personality which works like a computer's operating system. Within the first seven years of life, our Ego Self constructs patterns, program, rules, and beliefs. Our DNA, cultural conditioning, childhood experiences, and karma will all influence these constructs. Our Ego Self is our individuated self, and it has two primary desires: to stand out and to belong. Within your Ego Self, you have different identities or aspects of your personality and these all help to structure your day-to-day life.

These identities include archetypes, which are easily recognizable character types shared by many worldwide, regardless of culture. Archetypes are personality types that have been in our collective unconscious for centuries. We embody a number of them within ourselves. I identify myself as a mystic, artist, peacemaker, and mother, with a curious inner child. By describing my personality this way, I've painted a picture of myself for you to see, and so even if you've never met me in person, you might envision where I shop for groceries, what kind of car I drive, and even what I do for fun.

The concept of archetypes dates back to ancient times and the Greek philosopher Plato, but the 20th-century psychoanalyst Carl Jung introduced archetypes as we know them today. We see archetypal characters in all movies, myths, and stories. And you're already familiar with the hero, queen, damsel in distress, or clown. Certain archetypes are inherent within you, and they help your Ego Self individuate from others and make its mark on the world.

Circle those which resonate most with you.

Mother	Artist	Explorer
Father	Computer Geek	Outdoors Person
King	Oracle	Free-Spirit
Queen	Trickster	Athlete
Princess	Warrior	Coward
Prince	Slave	Dictator
Secretary	Hermit	Judge
Jokester or Clown	Teacher	Dilettante
Wounded Child	Doctor	Avenger
Boy	Healer	Seeker
Girl	Messenger	Student
Victim	Peacemaker	Shaman
Martyr	Monk	Patriarch
Hero	Prophet	Matriarch
Heroine	Servant	Jezebel
Mystic	Activist	Craftsperson
Visionary	Nun	Rescuer
Damsel in Distress	Crone	Good Samaritan
Villain	Maiden	Vampire
Magician	Diva	Fairy or Pixie
Priestess	Bully	Muse
Priest	Wizard	Knight
Lover	Witch	Boss
Prostitute	Starving Artist	Inventor
Saint	Caregiver	
Rebel	Fool	

Each of these archetypes, or personality types, has different needs and wants. So you can understand how your Ego Self might get confused from time to time. For this reason, it's important to enter the different parts of ourselves into a relationship with one another. And at the end of this chapter, I'll guide you through an exercise to help you have a dialog with the different aspects of your personality.

Subconscious Self

The Subconscious Self is your instinctual, embodied Self which remembers all the emotional imprints of your life experiences. It's nonverbal and primal. Your Subconscious Self has an important job to do; it keeps your physical systems going and makes sure you stay safe. So, it remembers everything, even when your conscious mind doesn't, and it is those memories associated with intense emotions that carry more meaning for your Subconscious Self.

Your Subconscious Mind, which links the mind and the body, wants to protect you and keep you alive. Emotions often signal thoughts and behaviors which fall under the domain of the Ego Self, but for you to access the full potential of your magical power, you'll need to feel safe in your body and in the world. So, all personal development involves working with your Subconscious Self to access its wisdom and assuage its concerns.

The Subconscious Self is the nonverbal part of yourself that thinks in metaphor and myth. You can access it through art, experiential therapies, somatic movement, dreams or meditative states, or storytelling. The next time you're in a Magic Crisis, practice the magical exercise, opposite, to find clues about how to restore your magical power.

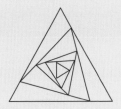

Talking to the Subconscious Self

1. Find a blank piece of paper and your favorite drawing utensil. You might want to play ambient music and have incense going as well. These can relax the senses and reinforce a sense of safety.

2. Take a deep breath and relax your body. Say in your mind: *In this moment, I am safe. I fully accept and embrace my subconscious self, and my heart is open as I go deeper into myself.*

3. Take another deep breath and close your eyes. Bring your awareness to your solar plexus, where your rib cage meets your diaphragm. Now, ask your Subconscious Self what it would like to share with you. Wait for the response.

4. With your drawing utensil in your non-dominant hand, draw images and symbols on the page. Relax with it! What shapes do you see? What images appear in your mind? If you *really* want to make it fun, use finger paints.

5. After five minutes, look at the page. What strikes you about the symbols before you? What do they mean? You might want to look at a dream dictionary for more clues and insights. Every shape will mean something and by exploring what these mean for you, you help your Subconscious Self to feel both seen and heard.

Journal Prompt

CHOOSE FOUR ARCHETYPES (SEE PAGE 65) THAT RESONATE THE MOST WITH YOU.

WHAT DOES EACH OF THESE ARCHETYPES HAVE TO SAY? ARE THERE ANY OTHER ARCHETYPES YOU EXPERIENCE IN YOUR PSYCHE? HOW CAN YOU WORK WITH THESE ARCHETYPES, SO THAT THEY CAN GET ALONG? ARE THERE ANY ASPECTS OF YOUR PERSONALITY HIDING IN THE SHADOWS? ANY YOU DON'T WANT TO ACCEPT? ARE THERE ANY ARCHETYPES YOU'D LIKE TO LET GO OF OR NEW ONES YOU'D LIKE TO ADOPT?

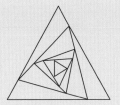

Write a Scene

Have you ever felt there are internal battles going on? Like part of you wants one thing and another part wants something else? You may even hear different voices in your mind. These desires come from different aspects of your personality. Enter them into a dialog with each other to help during those times you feel stuck.

Imagine you're a screenwriter developing a script about your primary intention. Give your script a title and write one short scene in which several of the different archetypes you've identified with meet to discuss your primary intention.

TITLE:
CHARACTERS:

The Ego Self:
Rules and Beliefs

The Ego Self holds your beliefs and the rules that structure your life experiences. Beliefs are thoughts that you've had over and over. Eventually, you adopt them as hard-wired facts, as the truth. But they can usually be disproven.

Think about something you believe to be true. On a scale of 1–10, how true is this belief? Do you know of instances in which it was proven untrue? For example, I grew up with the belief that you have to work hard to make money. Yet, I know of people who have wealth through inheritance or investments.

Why is it important to question our beliefs? Beliefs are like stones or boulders in the stream of our magical energy. If part of you believes you'll never succeed in fulfilling your primary intention, your magical energy will then flow in a different direction.

Our beliefs can become a code of rules we adopt, and rules can lead to self-punishment or resentment. I'll use my belief about money as an example. I believed money came through hard work. Anytime I took time off from work, my financial stress escalated. I had broken a rule, and I was unable to relax and have fun which was my self-punishment. My discovery of this belief led me to make significant changes and alter my experience of abundance. So, the good news is we can rewire this programming. The more conscious you are of your Ego Self's beliefs and rules, and the more willing you are to change your mind, the fewer boulders (beliefs) and obstacles you'll have in the flow of your magical energy.

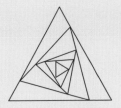

What Stands Between You and Your Intention?

1. In the stream of your magical energy, you might have a few stones or boulders (beliefs) guiding the flow. Reflect for a moment and envision yourself living the fulfillment of your primary intention. Can you see and feel that?

2. Now, look backward from that point. What obstacles did you have to overcome on your way to manifesting your primary intention?

3. List five ways you shifted each stone or boulder.

Get to Know Yourself to Trust Yourself

We experience all aspects of ourselves as a whole, and in Chapter 8, you'll learn specific integration techniques to align these different parts. First, you need to learn to viscerally "sense" and feel the different ways you experience each part of yourself. When your Higher Self speaks, how does it communicate with you? What about the aspects of your Ego Self? Which voice is which? When your Subconscious Self sends a signal, where can you locate it in your body?

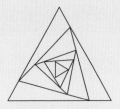

MAGICAL EXERCISE:

Experiencing the Different Aspects of Yourself

1. Take a deep breath and ground your energy. Draw your awareness into your navel. Say out loud: *Subconscious Self, I invite you to make yourself known to me. Let me feel you in my body.* Wait for the response. What do you feel? Where? Observe without judgment. Breathe and allow.

2. Next, draw your awareness to your solar plexus chakra. Say out loud: *Ego Self, I love and accept you. Please show yourself to me. Allow me to experience you through my physical senses. It is safe to do so. I will not abandon you.* What do you hear, see, or feel?

3. Draw your awareness into your heart center. Feel a smile at your heart center. Say out loud: *Higher Self, I invite you to make yourself known. How can I experience you in my body? How can I know you better? Come into my conscious awareness.* Take three deep breaths and relax your body.

4. Take five deep breaths and draw your awareness to the crown of your head. Tap it gently. Say out loud: *Divine Self, I invite you to make yourself known to me. Allow me to feel and experience you.* Breathe deeply, allowing yourself to experience your Divine Self with all senses.

5. When you feel complete, draw your awareness down to your feet and ground yourself (see page 74). Open your eyes.

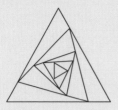

MAGICAL EXERCISE:

Grounding

Grounding is important because it allows us to be present in our bodies and to better differentiate between the various aspects of ourselves. It also helps us connect with the earth and the natural world where we witness our magic working in our lives. Here are three ways to ground and center:

BE IN NATURE
Step outside and feel the air, touch the earth, feel the sun's heat, or let the moon's rays shine down on you. If you are near a water element, dip your hands in and sense the water. Observe what you see without labeling, classifying, or judging anything. Just experience nature as she shows herself to you.

MINI SQUATS
Stand and bounce up and down, doing several mini squats. This exercise charges your root chakra, the energy center of your body that is connected to the earth.

VISUALIZATION
With your feet firmly on the ground, visualize strong roots leading from your feet to the core of the earth. See these roots going down deep beneath the layers of the earth. Breathe in the earth's nourishment as you connect.

Magic Rule #2 :

Magic
Is
Power

5

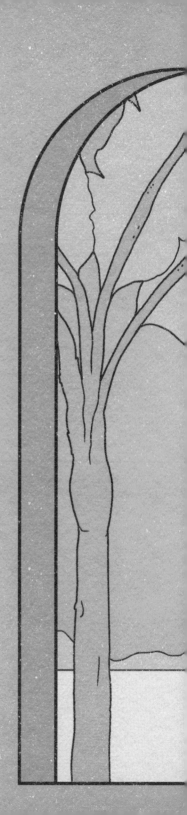

In what ways would your life look different if you felt more powerful? Many of us grew up believing we don't have much authority over what happens in our lives. And when you're in a Magic Crisis, you often feel helpless to affect any positive change in your life. But we only feel powerless when we forget that we're masterful creators of our life experiences—when we feel as if our futures are in the hands of unseen forces way beyond and outside of ourselves. None of this is true; no matter what you've survived, you will always have the power to shape your life. Magic is an equal-opportunity power—one that we all have the right to experience, regardless of gender, privilege, or economic status.

This chapter invites you to live a more powerful life. Discover how to embody your power and deepen your experience of it. You'll also begin to see how you've yielded power to others, and why you might fear your own power.

Daily Practice

Make a list of people who embody power to you. Who are your models of power, and why? Add to the list each day, identifying what aspects of that individual you see in yourself.

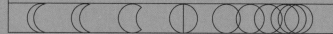

You Are Powerful

Magic is your power to create and connect. Magic is an inherent power. It's within you, but it's also a power—a spirit—you access each time you speak an intention into the heart of the Divine. It's supernatural because *you* are supernatural, and within the supernatural exists everything that is natural. It's embodied, sensed, and shared. To experience magic as power, we must first define power for ourselves. What is it? Where does it come from? Who has it? Who doesn't? Let's take a look ...

Power

The Latin root of the word power, *potere*, means "to be able." Power is your presence. It's your embodied spirit. It encompasses your feelings, preferences, strengths, skills, perspective, voice, and contribution to the world. It's your ability: what you can and can't do.

When I think of power, I think of electricity. Miles of power lines connect your home to an electrical substation in the city. Your home has a main circuit breaker with connected wires that run throughout your house. So, when you turn on a light, you open the flow of electricity from the primary source to the light. The light isn't power. It uses the power, but the power is the source. Your power is not:

A. Your ability to dominate others.
B. Your ability to intimidate others.
C. Your physical strength to attack others.
D. Your ability to manipulate others and have them bend to your will.

Your power is your "You" essence; it's your spark. It's what makes you shine your light in the world, and each one of us expresses our power differently.

Power Is Multifaceted

The power we described above is different from a hierarchical power based on control and domination. Power "over" has been the predominant power structure for patriarchal institutions, like religion and government. It's shaped our culture and our understanding of power. The more privilege you have, the easier it is to use your voice, make decisions, establish boundaries, and state your preferences. Privilege from this hierarchical power structure gives you more freedom to be yourself and pursue happiness.

And what happens in a macrocosm happens in a microcosm because our family systems mirror societal ones. In childhood, we learn to experience our inherent power within these systems. We test our boundaries and learn how safe it is to assert ourselves, make choices, or shine our light in the world. You might have learned to fear or suppress your power. As a result, you will have become accustomed to a comfort zone.

Think about this in terms of setting intentions and focusing your magical power in a ritual or spell. If you grow up believing your thoughts matter, being encouraged to express your voice and receiving opportunities to do so, you might state your intentions with faith and conviction. Your life experiences have given you reasons to trust your magical power. If you felt powerless and helpless throughout childhood, you might find you now have a more limited comfort zone of power in adulthood.

I like to envision my comfort zone as a giant glass box that surrounds my body. Whenever I press up against the boundaries of my comfort zone, everything inside me feels tight and constricted. It takes courage to crack the glass, stretch wider, and grow.

The good news is that once you shatter the glass walls, you'll have a hard time shrinking back down. Throughout your life, you will become more powerful and learn to shine your light more brightly.

What If I'm Afraid of My Power?

I remember a time when I felt powerless. I was so afraid to disappoint others, and I had made life decisions according to what my loved ones would accept. One night, sitting on the floor in the corner of my bathroom, sobbing, I realized I could no longer ignore the whisper in my heart urging me to leave my marriage. The life I had been living wasn't my own, but one I'd wanted so badly to fit. I tried very hard to make it work, but in doing so, I'd abandoned myself. Restoring a sense of power meant saying the words I'd been holding back for so long; the ones that would alienate me from my family and friends and topple the stable life I'd built—I'm a lesbian.

In what ways will your life change when you embody more power? Are you afraid of those changes? Would staying just where you are right now feel any better?

With more presence and power, you will feel freer to make decisions, even if they're unpopular: decisions like leaving a relationship, walking away from a job, or writing a memoir. The more agency you have in your life, the more you affect change in your familial and social circles. By being more magical, your life may change in both big and small ways. Should you be afraid of your power to change your life? Only if you want to stay exactly where you are right now. (Hint: You wouldn't be reading this book if you did!)

Given our historical and societal experiences of power, it's only natural you may have a little (or big) fear of your magical power. After all, we were burned at the stake for this stuff not too many centuries ago. However, the time to reclaim, own, and embody your power is now!

If you're afraid of your power, you need to expand your comfort zone. You need to push out those glass walls, raise the ceiling, and start getting more comfortable in the expanded space of power. Fear is natural; letting it stop you is not.

No matter what childhood experiences or life events shaped your comfort zone, you can stretch it and expand beyond the bounds of its current limits. The exercise on the following page will help you do just that.

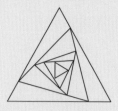

MAGICAL EXERCISE:

Expanding Your Comfort Zone

1. Stand in a way that feels comfortable. Think about your primary intention. What happens to your breath? What do you notice in your body? This state of being is your current comfort zone. Does it feel tight? Open?

2. Take a deep breath. State your intention. Where in your body do you feel tight? That is your inner *no*.

3. Place your hands at your chest, facing away from your body. Feeling your *no*, push your hands out several inches away. In your mind, hear and feel *yes*. Keep pushing until you only feel your *yes*.

4. Repeat this exercise to either side of your body.

5. With hands facing towards the sky, think of your primary intention. Feel it in your heart. Feel the *no* of where it is right now. Now, you're going to raise your own ceiling.

6. Push your hands up slowly and say the word *yes* in your mind. Once your hands are up as high as they can go, have a good stretch.

7. Turn around inside your new comfort zone. Feel it expand around you as you move in whatever ways your body feels led to move. Embody your power.

Your whole life is a dance of expansion and contraction, but the more you allow yourself to push beyond your comfort zone, the more powerful you become in your life and the world.

Who Has Your Power?

If you were to see your heart from your soul's perspective, you would see a whole network of cords like telephone lines connecting your heart to the hearts of others. From time to time, you may inadvertently send energy through those cords. When you think of someone, that cord lights up, and your energy flows toward them. They likely feel it too and send you energy in return by thinking of you. The more energy someone receives, the more power they feel.

When we work with magic, we need to have full access to that energy. If you aim your focus at others, like your ex or the politician you despise, you need to draw it all back into yourself, at least while you're involved in magical practices.

Journal Prompt

WHAT CHANGES COULD I MAKE IN MY LIFE TO FEEL MORE POWERFUL?

HOW DOES MY EXPERIENCE OF SOCIO-ECONOMIC POWER AFFECT MY INHERENT PERSONAL POWER?

WHAT MESSAGES HAVE I RECEIVED ABOUT MY ABILITY TO ASSERT MYSELF AND MAKE LIFE CHOICES?

IN THE PAST, HAVE I YIELDED MY POWER TO A PERSON OR INSTITUTION? WHAT PURPOSE DID THAT SERVE?

HOW AM I YIELDING POWER NOW?

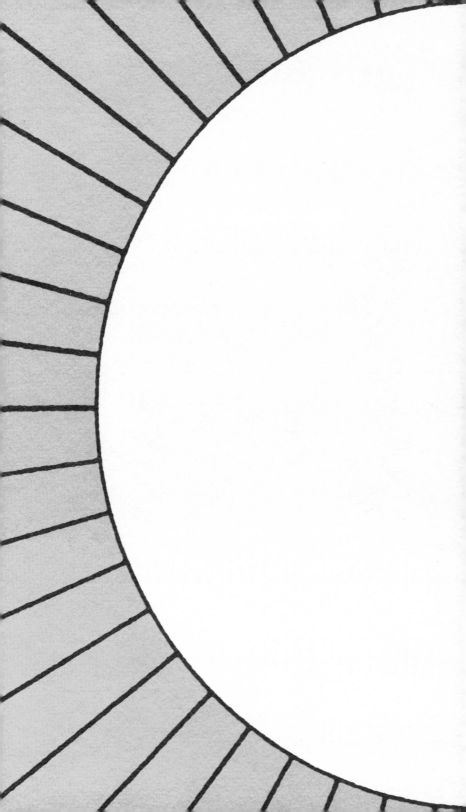

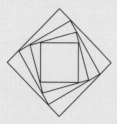

RITUAL:

Reclaim Your Power

In this ritual, you will draw all of your heartstrings—those energetic cords—back to yourself. Rather than cutting those cords, you're going to lovingly, gently pull them back to you. You will need a white candle for this ritual, purifying incense (I like frankincense or myrrh), and crystals that correspond to the heart. Some of my favorite crystals for this ritual include clear quartz, rose quartz, amethyst, apophyllite, aquamarine, aventurine, bloodstone, emerald, malachite, rhodochrosite, and rhodonite.

Visualize yourself surrounded by light, your Aura Globe (see page 58). Light the white candle and say:

> *At this moment, within this hour,*
> *I reclaim my power*
> *With grace and love.*
> *I draw into myself*
> *What was and is and always will be mine.*
> *I give back to others*
> *What was and is and always will be theirs.*
> *I embody my power.*
> *I am my power.*

Visualize your heartstrings. Gather them all in a bunch at your heart center, and then pull them into your chest. Sit in meditation for a moment and feel your power return to you.

Hold your crystal in your palm and charge it with your power so it becomes a representation of your inherent power, presence, and love.

Power
Through Fear

When fear occupies our minds, we don't feel as powerful in our lives or magical practices. If you're preoccupied with worries, your magic is flowing in their direction.

Every thought is a magical spell. Each one plants a seed of intention. The ones you feed with attention and emotion establish roots and grow.

LET'S PUT THIS INTO PRACTICE:

Take a deep breath, and ask yourself: What is my primary intention, my heart's deep desire?

Close your eyes and picture it. Lean into that vision of your fulfilled intention and fully experience it. Don't judge it as being good or bad, right or wrong. Your heart deserves the chance to feel that intention. Again, what is your intention?

Own it. Even if it doesn't come to fruition in the way you expect right now, you will use that intention to better understand and feel magic coursing through your life. State it with vigor! Own your intention. As you do, you reclaim and embody your power. Focus and attention both help manifest intention but what percentage of you wants to manifest this intention? Answer honestly. If it's only 10 percent, that's useful information.

Center all your awareness in your heart. Disengage your mind. Ask again: What percentage of you wants to manifest this intention? Experience that feeling, that deep longing and desire. Ask where that desire comes from: Divine Self, Higher Self, Ego Self, Subconscious Self.

What aspects of you don't believe you deserve to manifest that intention? How can those aspects of you embody more power? Answer with the first response. Right now, we are merely gathering information that you will work with throughout the next few chapters.

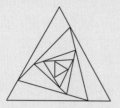

MAGICAL EXERCISE:

Find the Fear

Sometimes, we can identify our fears. Other times, we only have evidence of them because we're distracted, checked out, or frustrated. Fear can be tricky. It likes to hide beneath layers of other feelings or thoughts. There is often a deep-seated root of fear lurking in the shadows, but when you find it, you can call it up and diminish its power.

When you see evidence of fear because you've gotten distracted or frustrated, ask: "What is my fear?" Take a moment to tune in. Silence yourself and listen. Once you answer the question, you might experiment with going deeper. Keep asking the question until you have a breakthrough.

What is your fear?
Does that feel entirely true? If not, ask again.
When you have an answer, ask again. What is your fear?
Does that feel entirely true? If not, ask again.
What is your fear?

Keep asking until you get to a core truth that resonates deeply within you. It will feel like a mic-drop moment, and it might give you chills. I'll give you an example of how it went for me when trying to conceive a child:

What is your fear?
> *That I won't become a mother.*

Does that feel entirely true?
> *Not really.*

What is your fear?
> *That I won't be a good mother.*

Does that feel entirely true?
> *Somewhat, but not entirely.*

What is your fear?
> *That motherhood is too hard.*

Does that feel entirely true?
> *It feels somewhat true.*

What is your fear?
> *That I'll leave my child.*

Does that feel entirely true?
> *It feels very close to true, but something's missing.*

What is your fear?
> *That I'll die and leave my child alone.*

Mic drop! That one struck a chord. When I found myself writing that fear, I couldn't believe it. Where did it come from? How had it made its way into my psyche? When I was able to see the hidden fear, I could then disengage from it. It didn't have power anymore, and most importantly, it didn't feel real. Sometimes, that's all you have to do—bring the fear into the light.

You don't always have to know where the fear is coming from, whether it stemmed from a past life or childhood experience or whether it's an intuition about the future. Acknowledge it, have compassion for yourself, and let it dissolve away.

Attention renders fear inept. When you have that mic-drop moment, that's when you know you've uncovered the root of your fears.

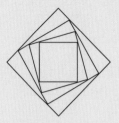

RITUAL:

Transmuting Fear

In the following ritual, you will transmute this fear, stirring it into the cauldron. You'll need:

Your cauldron	Yellow or white candles	A touchstone such as
Water	Incense such as myrrh or	clear quartz crystal
Salt	frankincense (or both)	Magic wand

1. Light your candle, calling in your divine helper. Light the incense to begin to open your senses. Half-fill your cauldron with water. (Distilled or filtered water is the best, but you can use tap water, too.)

2. Hold the touchstone, and imagine your fear leaving your body through your hands and into the stone. State the word *fear* three times, and each time, feel it leave your body.

3. What would you like your fear to morph into? Peace? Motivation? Love? Grace? Name and claim it.

4. Fill the cauldron with salt so that there is one part salt to two parts water. With your magic wand, stir the salt and say:

    Take my fear
    Dissolve it away
    In its place, fill my heart with
    (State what you'd like fear to morph into)

I am free from the ties that bind.
Free to love, live, and be
My true Divine Self.

5. Say this over and over, stirring until the salt has dissolved. Then, place the touchstone in the salt water, letting it sit in the water for clearing.

6. You can meditate for a moment with your palms held over the water for extra healing. When you feel complete, take the touchstone out of the water and dry it off. Run it through the incense and pass it over the candle, blessing it as you do.

7. When you feel complete, extinguish the candle and close the circle (see pages 175–177). You can flush the salt water down the toilet or pour it into the ground.

Magic Rule #3 :

Attention
Is
Power

Working with magic requires concentration, but not just mental concentration; it's a whole-body, whole-spirit concentration. After all, attention is power. Practice as much as possible, even when you're not doing magic, to fine-tune your skills.

In this chapter, we will talk about the power of attention and why we become so easily distracted. I will share some simple concentration exercises that you can then do when your mind races or you feel preoccupied.

Daily Practice

Meditate for at least 10 minutes and pay attention to your breath.

Inhale for four counts and exhale for four counts.

If your mind starts to wander, bring your focus back to your breath.

Try this with a sitting or walking meditation.

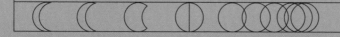

Magic = Power
Attention = Power
Your Attention =
Powerful Magic!

When you focus your attention, you send waves of your energy—your magical power—to whatever is preoccupying your thoughts.

When you hold onto resentment or blame, you send waves of your power—your magic—to the person or situation that initially hurt you. You're giving a little of your *juju* to that person, place, or thing. It's one thing to acknowledge and accept your feelings. It's another to ruminate in those emotions in a way that limits your access to your power.

A Thought Is a Magical Spell

If you think the same thing over and over again, that thought becomes a magic spell. Your thoughts are like radio signals broadcasting to the world, and soon they can become intentions—intentional or unintentional ones.

I experimented with this concept by thinking affirmative thoughts and observing what feedback I received from others. Each day for several weeks, I would focus on the thought: "I've lost weight!" (I hadn't lost weight.) I woke up thinking that idea, maintained it throughout the day, and fell asleep thinking it. Soon after, three friends asked if I had lost weight. It worked! Within a few weeks, I'd lost three pounds without even trying. That slight weight loss motivated me to adopt healthier habits, and over time, I lowered my normal weight by five pounds.

Energy follows attention

If you want to feel better about your finances, give attention to your successes and celebrate the abundance you experience in your life. If you want to feel better about your career, focus on what you appreciate about your work right now. If you want to be more magical, aim your attention at what feels like magic in your life. Focus on performing everyday rituals and on being open to seeing signs and wonders in your environment.

Attention is a function of both mind and body. All aspects of ourselves have attention to focus, and when they're all aimed in one direction, we can make powerful magic!

MAGICAL EXERCISE:

The Magic Dot

1. What is your intention? Draw a black dot and concentrate on it.

2. In this dot, write your intention with black ink. If you do it well, you shouldn't be able to see any words. As you write, feel it in your heart. You can write it over and over to master concentration. You can try this exercise if you lose focus at work or your mind starts drifting. You can also use it as a helpful tool when moving through doubt or uncertainty.

When you focus on disappointment, you direct your magical power away from your intention and slip into doubt. Doubt can shake our confidence or cause us to feel less powerful. It serves a purpose, though. You cannot arrive at faith without moving through the swampy waters of doubt. Likewise, we can't access courage without feeling fear. In facing our fears, we become braver.

Whatever you feed with your attention grows. When you're in a Magic Crisis, notice where your thoughts go; what you're reading online; or how you're spending your time, energy, and money. These will all give you clues about what's benefiting from your attention—your magical power.

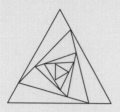

MAGICAL EXERCISE:

Find Your Center

When you feel scattered, you can always bring yourself back to center. This exercise will help.

1. Take a deep breath. As you exhale, feel any tension in your body relax. Draw your awareness into the center of your chest behind your sternum. Feel the expansiveness of that space as you relax your mind and body.

2. Allow your awareness to move down into your solar plexus beneath your rib cage above your stomach. Feel the expanse of that space as you deepen your awareness. Say to yourself: *I am centered. I feel safe and know I'm loved.*

3. Say it again and again until the words feel true.

4. Think of that space behind your sternum as a gateway into your spiritual center—your soul. If you relax and allow your imagination to take over, you might even feel as if there's a whole universe within you. You can achieve a sort of transcendence *within* yourself to feel at one with your Divine Self in your body.

5. Now, relax your awareness and ask yourself: Where do I feel my center?

6. Journal your observations and practice returning to this space often. There's a universe of knowledge, information, and guidance there for you.

Amulets, Tinctures, and Potions

When you make things like amulets, tinctures, and potions, you have a specific focus for your attention. When you create a sacred space, focus all of your attention on an intention, and engage in a creative process, then you're using your magical power to the fullest.

MAGICAL EXERCISE:

Make a Magical Symbol

A sigil is a magical symbol, and it works! Start by writing your intention. Remember to keep it simple and specific. Cross out all of the vowels. Then, cross out all of the duplicate consonants. You should have a group of consonants on the paper before you. Here's where you get to use your creativity. Start by drawing the first consonant. Then, connect the second consonant to the first in a way that looks good to you. Do the same with the third, connecting it to the second. Continue this process until you have used all the letters. Here is an example. Let's use the intention:

I experience the fullness of my magical power in my everyday life.

Now, let's cross off all vowels.
I̶ experi̶enc̶e̶ the̶ fu̶llne̶ss o̶f my ma̶gi̶ca̶l po̶we̶r i̶n my e̶ve̶ryda̶y li̶fe̶.

Let's cross off the duplicate consonants.
I̶ e̶xpe̶ri̶e̶nce̶ the̶ fullne̶ss o̶f my ma̶gi̶ca̶l po̶we̶r i̶n my e̶ve̶ryda̶y li̶fe̶.

Now, we're left with the letters: XPRNCTHFLSMGWVD

Let's make a symbol from these letters. We'll start with X, then add P, then R, and so on. You can be creative with this process. End up with a drawing that makes you feel the power of your intention each time you look at it.

Use Your Magic Wand

You can use your magic wand to help focus your attention too. Just as some people use a mantra during meditation, so you can use your magic wand to center yourself by holding and sensing it in your hands.

When you're using your magic wand in a ritual, you can focus all of your energy on one end of it. Then, visualize that energy moving through the wand and out to your intention on the other end. It helps if you aim your wand at a symbol of your intention. After you draw a magical symbol, feel the emotions you'll have when your intention comes to fruition. Place the tip of your magic wand on the symbol. Let the energy you're generating swell up in your heart and move it through the palms of your hands as you hold your wand. Visualize that energy moving through your magic wand and out into the symbol itself. Hold the intensity until you feel it rise. Then, in a long exhale, let go.

Attention Is Power

When you shift your attention from the present moment, you give your power to that distracting thought. Your power is your vital, life-force energy—your *juju!* It's the energy you'll use to change your life.

I'll let you in on a secret. I get easily distracted. I want to focus all of my attention and power on the task of writing this paragraph. As I write it, I find my attention (my power) shifting from the book to my shopping list to a text message to my email. Why do I scatter my attention onto so many different things when I want to write this paragraph more than anything else? The answer lies in the subtle subconscious aspects of the self and we need to do a deep dive to explore why we become so distracted and what we can do about it.

You have a multitude of wants and desires at any moment. To focus your full attention in a magical practice like a ritual or spell, you want to quieten those other distracting wants and desires. Maybe you feel scattered with too much going on all at once.

One of the reasons you can fall into a Magic Crisis is the very busyness of day-to-day life. Soon, you feel more disconnected from yourself and separated from your power. You have maximum use of your power in this present moment. Being truly present in your body is the foundation for magical work. So, if your back starts hurting all of a sudden, or you remember something you forgot to pick up at the store, gently return your attention to the present moment and your Magical Practice.

So, how do you focus on one and release all the other wants? However, when I asked you: "What is your primary intention?" you thought of one primary, but then four more probably popped into your mind. When you focus on one, you can begin to rest in that desire, settle your spirit, and trust. Let's try.

1. Think about your primary intention. Can you feel it in your heart? What is the primary emotion associated with that intention?

2. Draw your awareness into your heart. Does all of you want this primary intention? Answer quickly with the first response you feel.

3. If the answer is no, what aspect of you does not want this primary intention? What aspects of you want this primary intention?

4. When you long for something so badly that it burns in your heart, you can trust that desire comes from your higher self, and it will lead to your highest good.

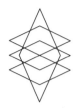

Intention + Attention = Focused Magical Power

To better focus your power, strengthen your will which is effectively your *yes* to your desires. You experience your will in your heart as enthusiasm. The stronger your will, the more passionate you feel and the more committed you'll be. Think of it like this:

Your will = your "yes" to what you most desire.
Your will = your decision-making power

Beliefs, fears, thoughts, and conditions can all weaken our will. You'll know part of you is distracted when you state your intention and then hear in your mind:

But ... What if ... I can't ...

When these distractions come into your conscious awareness, write them down to diffuse their power. What is your primary intention? What distracts your attention away from your intention? Nothing brings us into focus like an intense emotion, and when I work with magic I like to generate the feeling of enthusiasm to help focus my attention.

Say your intention over and over and feel it in your heart. Hear the power of your voice as you speak with conviction. Cheer yourself on! You can also do this with another person and generate enthusiasm for one another's intentions.

Now, be powerful. Declare your intention from a state of certainty and knowing. Feel the power of your *yes* coursing through your body. Expect it will happen and allow no space for other factors.

Putting It All Together

1. Feel the desire in your heart.

2. If you feel tension or find yourself holding your breath, you have some resistance to the fulfillment of that desire. If so, keep breathing.

3. Know whether it is your Divine Self, Higher Self, Ego Self, or Subconscious Self that wants the desire.

4. Locate the aspects of yourself that resist and find out why. (Hint: It's usually fear.)

5. Love and accept all of you, even those resistant parts.

6. Breathe, relax, and let go.

Letting Go

There's a big difference between focused attention and obsession. When we obsess about a desire, we can develop unhealthy attachments to the outcomes we want and thus limit the flow of magic. When you're working with magic, you want to focus on your ritual, spell, or other activity and then just let go. Ask yourself:

In what areas of your life are you gripping tightly right now?
Where in your body are you resisting the flow of breath?

By bringing your breath into the tight areas of your body, you can influence a shift in your life circumstances.

It's challenging to let go of a passionate unmet desire. Powerful emotions command our attention. When you've experienced a loss, for example, your mind continues to rewind to the painful event you experienced. After a breakup, job loss, death of a loved one, health diagnosis, or accident, we ruminate about the series of choices that led to the event as a way of trying to go back in time to achieve a different outcome. But this game of mental gymnastics we play can lead to even more pain and greater despair.

Letting go means surrendering to the Divine and the forces of magic. We'll talk more about this in Chapter 9, but in the meantime, here are some simple steps you can take when attention moves toward obsession.

THE FOUR STEPS OF LETTING GO:

Step One:	**Relax**
Step Two:	**Breathe**
Step Three:	**Show Gratitude**
Step Four:	**Open Your Heart**

Relax

Take a moment to release the tension in your body. Find the tight places, tense them up, and then let go of that tension. Feel relaxation move into those muscles. Let your jaw relax. Unclench your teeth. Shake your arms and feel the energy move out through your hands. Clap your hands. Stomp your feet. Shake your legs and wiggle your torso. Move that tension out, out, out, and away.

Breathe

Deep breathing can activate your parasympathetic nervous system and help the brain relax. It can slow mental chatter or wild thoughts because it brings more oxygen to the brain. Breathing can stimulate more feel-good hormones and physiological responses. Inhale into your diaphragm for four counts, feeling your breath down in your stomach and lower back. Hold that breath for two counts and exhale for five counts. Hold that exhaled breath for two counts and repeat the whole series several times.

Show Gratitude

When you're feeling stressed, traumatized, or angry about your life circumstances, you are far from feeling grateful. It might feel good to stay angry or sad when you're moving through the initial shock of loss or pain. If someone has hurt you, you might feel vindicated by holding onto anger or resentment. So, in no way am I telling you what to feel or how to respond to life's events. I get it! I have been there, too. And because I've been there, I know that when you are ready to let go and move into a different chapter of the experience, gratitude is your key. It's not enough to list what you're grateful for. You've got to feel it with your whole heart. Bask in it. Let every cell reverberate with it.

Think about the most challenging life circumstance you're facing right now. Find one beautiful aspect of that situation. You might feel a sting as you discover your heart is expansive enough to hold both gratitude and grief. Don't look away or shift your focus. Explore that life circumstance from all angles and focus on the beauty.

Open Your Heart

Painful experiences can either break us wide open or cause our fragile hearts to close down out of a need for safety and protection. To open your heart, take a few deep breaths and center your awareness at your heart center. In your mind, say:, "I open and allow goodness to flow into my heart at this time." Visualize a bright light shining at your heart center. Stretch your arms behind you and physically open your chest, relieving tension as you stretch. Roll your shoulders back and forth and feel all of the muscles surrounding your heart open and relax.

To open your heart even wider than this, repeat *Step Three: Gratitude* which will expand your heart's capacity to receive love. Regularly practice gratitude with an open heart, and you'll start to experience more love in your life and more magic too.

These four simple steps have helped me release the grip of control when I've lived through some unpleasant experiences or unwanted outcomes. During those times, we need to rely on all of the magic tools in our toolboxes.

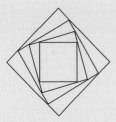

RITUAL:

Letting Go

Some circumstances and losses are so upsetting that we need to create a ritual to honor the event or person and say goodbye. A simple Letting Go ritual I like to use goes like this:

1. Light a white candle. As you do, say what you're letting go out loud three times.

2. Place your hands on either side of the candle (far enough away from the flame to avoid burning yourself). Imagine sending the energy you're holding in your body from your heart and mind out through your hands. Imagine it moving into the fire and rising into the smoke. Hold this sensation for several minutes until you feel a release.

3. Exhale deeply without blowing out the candle. Then, feel the warmth of the flame moving through your hands, up your arms, and into your heart.

4. Imagine light filling your whole body and clearing any residual energy from the situation that you just let go. Take some deep breaths and say, *I allow light into all empty spaces. I am whole and wholly present for goodness to flow into my life. My heart is open.*

5. When you feel complete, snuff out the candle using a candle snuffer or something similar.

Magic Rule #4 :

Embrace
Your
Dark
Side

7

Welcome to my favorite chapter—the one about embracing your dark side. If you've ever been depressed, lost, confused, grief-stricken, or passionate, or find yourself yearning for something, this chapter is for you. Your dark side is powerful and magical. In this chapter, we enter into the hidden, unconscious part of you and cozy up to your dark side so you can draw on the power of the dark to nurture your magical acts. I'll show you the tools and exercises you'll need to help you fall in love with your dark side so you will see it as your helper rather than a saboteur.

Daily Practice

Say this forgiveness prayer at least once a day:

To all who have hurt me: I forgive you.
I love you and thank you for the valuable lessons.
To all whom I have caused suffering through
my words, acts, or deeds: I'm sorry.
Please forgive me.
I love you. Blessed Be.

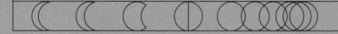

Embracing the Dark

Being powerful allows you to feel safe in the world. When you're powerful, you're unshakable and centered to the core. You know your preferences and aren't afraid to state them. You can feel your emotions. You love yourself enough to honor those preferences and not judge your own emotions. You also know your limits and dare to set boundaries. Being powerful means that you won't abandon yourself to earn the acceptance of someone else. It means being brave—not because you don't feel fear, but rather, you know how to use fear as fuel to propel an act of courage. Being powerful means risking rejection, failure, or loss. It means seeing yourself as the universe's co-conspirator and not a victim of circumstances.

"But what does all this have to do with my dark side?"

Well, we can't be powerful if we suppress or repress any part of ourselves. We can't be powerful if we feel like a victim of circumstances in our lives.

Embracing your dark side means two things:

1. Loving your whole self. Love the parts you don't want to see—the parts that have been hiding in the shadows.

2. Loving the people, places, and things that have caused you the most suffering, pain, and loss.

But Isn't My Dark Side Evil and Scary?

Your light isn't more spiritual than your dark. It's not a higher vibe, purer energy, or more God-like. Your dark side isn't evil, depressed, violent, or prurient. Think of your dark side as the wild, untamed part of yourself; it's your raw emotion, passion, sensuality, and sexuality. It's your fecundity. The dark is the part of us that draws energy from the earth and communes with nature. It's nonlinear, fluid, and subtle. It's the womb—the seat of creative power (and this applies even if you don't, literally, have a uterus).

We have learned to fear our dark side, but when we learn to embrace it, we discover our ferocity, wildness, and joy. Suppressed, turned in on itself, feared, or unloved, darkness mutates into something other than what it is. Then, it can, in fact, become self-defeating, depressed, abusive, or even violent.

Our ancient forefathers informed the dualistic thinking that has permeated our culture, and it is within this framework that we began to differentiate and polarize:

Light from dark.
Good from evil.
Right from wrong.
Male from female.
Reason from emotion.

Visibility from hiddenness.
Action from passivity.
Chastity from sexuality.
Spirit from matter.
Heaven from earth.

Within this framework, light is to good as dark is to evil. Dualistic thinking has influenced cultures for centuries (well, really, since the inception of patriarchal times) and within this polarity lies a hierarchy. Because men were the ones telling the stories, we learned to prize and give privilege to the masculine—spirit, reason, light, and God. Because it was woven into our collective consciousness, we learned to judge everything in our lives according to this construct. In the process, we developed a sense of separation from our bodies, the earth, and one another.

What if the "Devil" isn't some bad guy out to tempt you? What if he's the mythological Horned God of nature, wilderness, and sexuality? He brings souls into the underworld after they've passed. And maybe the underworld isn't *hell* as we've come to think of it—all fire and brimstone. What if it is a sacred space that we enter between lives? Like a fertile womb where we're nurtured and healed before our next incarnation.

This is the place where we purify ourselves of past wrongdoing, and so what if our demons aren't out to get us? Instead, they could be projections of our unmet fears, some of which we may have inherited from our ancestors? If we ask ourselves these questions and disrupt our beliefs about demons, devils, and other spiritual entities, then we can finally work with magic without fear. If we have nothing to fear, nothing can control us. And that's how we become more powerful.

A dualistic construct of reality requires us to play a constant balancing act within ourselves and our relationships. If we have learned to give privilege to the *yang* or masculine, we might find ourselves leaning in that direction. We might talk ourselves out of feeling emotions rather than letting them be a source of power. We may seesaw between the two impulses, never feeling whole or integrated within ourselves.

To be powerful and magical, we need to stop this balancing act by accepting all of ourselves and loving and living holistically. But how do we do that?

We are, collectively, beginning to shift away from dualistic thinking. We can, for example, thank our gender-fluid friends for helping us rethink binary gender constructs. And if we can step out of the dualistic framework as it pertains to masculinity and femininity, then we can imagine Heaven and Earth as one. We can see God and the Devil and the Goddess alive in all of creation. We can then allow ourselves to imagine a culture that's neither matriarchal nor patriarchal, but rather one that's universal and whole again.

Love Is the
Great Unifier?

If we are to reclassify these polarities, let's imagine putting one big blanket over all of it. Call that blanket "Love". If we see all as love—the pain and suffering, as well as the joy—we can suspend judgment of good or bad. Instead, we can ask questions like:

What is love trying to teach me through this?
How can I see this heartbreak as love?
How does love see this other person?
What would love do right now?
What does love want for my work? My family?
My community?
What does love want for my country?

Love is the divine source that works in and through you, others, and the natural world, and it encompasses the dark, the light, and the shades in between.

Journal Prompt

THINK OF YOUR PRIMARY INTENTION. THEN ANSWER THE FOLLOWING QUESTIONS;

WHAT DOES LOVE WANT ME TO KNOW?

WHAT DOES LOVE WANT ME TO DO NEXT?

WHO DOES LOVE WANT ME TO REACH OUT TO FOR GUIDANCE OR SUPPORT?

WHAT DOES LOVE WANT TO SHOW ME ABOUT MY PRIMARY INTENTION?

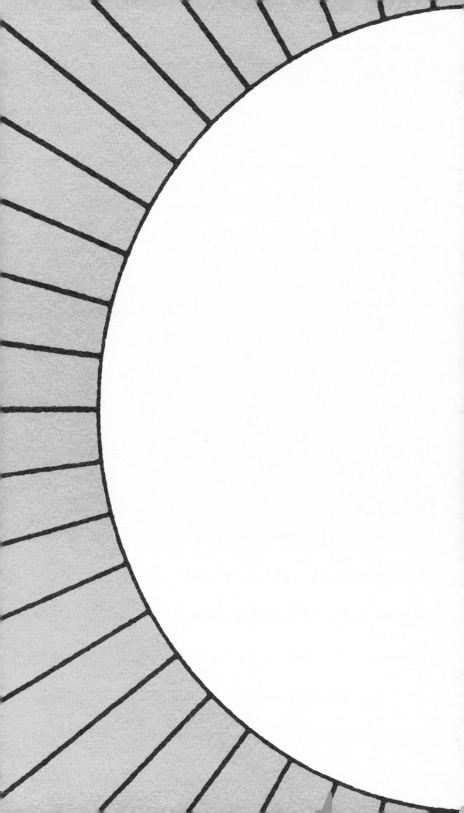

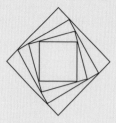

Let in the Love

For this ritual, you'll need your magic wand and your touchstones. Sit in a comfortable position as close to the ground as possible. I recommend sitting outside if you can.

1. Place your touchstones around your body to create a sacred circle. Visualize a small purifying fire outside your circle.

2. With your magic wand aimed towards that fire, send all fear into its flames. Bring all awareness into your heart. Aim your magic wand toward your heart and invoke your divine helpers by saying:

   I fill my entire being with love. I forgive myself and others. I forgive the forces of nature. I forgive the universe. I fully and completely accept myself and my life, and I open myself to the grace of the Divine. I am love, and I love.

3. Set your magic wand down and place your palms flat on the ground. Draw energy up from the earth and return the love.

4. When you finish, put out the imaginary fire, close your circle (see pages 180–181) and say "thank yous" to your divine helpers.

Embracing the Dark Times in Life

Things like natural disasters, accidents, illness, the sudden loss of a loved one, or economic setbacks can leave us feeling powerless. When the unthinkable happens, we feel abandoned and left alone to face a harsh reality. We feel abandoned by our divine helpers and, thus, separated from the spiritual sources of love.

Believe it or not, it is during the most trying times in our lives that we become supernatural. Our power reverberates throughout our bodies and moves out into the world, although we're often unable to feel it. Significant losses put our Ego Self to rest long enough for our Higher Self to step in and restructure our lives according to what would most fulfill our soul's calling.

The Ego Self doesn't like to rest and in those difficult times, you may feel like dying or even wish you were dead. You're not dying—you're in the middle of a magical process. Celebrate it! Say to yourself, "My Ego Self is under construction." Reach out to others for help because we are not meant to suffer alone.

Try to accept precisely where you are and to trust and know that it will get better. Seek help if necessary. Your dark thoughts mean you're in the fertile underworld—the womb of the Goddess. There's a creation process happening, and when you emerge, think of how much more enriched your life will be!

The most painful and traumatic circumstances of our lives are pathways to power. In moving through those dark times, we face our greatest fears and limiting beliefs. If we want to feel better, we have no choice but to allow in more love. By doing so, we're more receptive to support, connection, poetry, beauty, grace, and expressions of love and we can then allow miracles to unfold and magic to happen.

How Do I Allow in More Love?

Love is an abstract idea, isn't it? It's difficult to grasp or define, much less to conjure up at a moment's notice. It's also a construct. Each of us has a different idea of what love is or isn't from our childhood experiences, spiritual beliefs, and cultural conditioning. But how can we allow more of something we can't even clearly define into our lives?

Love is not just an emotion; it's pure divine energy. So, when we talk about letting love in, we're talking about receiving an outpouring of the spiritual forces of love. You might call this force the Goddess, God, Allah, the Holy Spirit, or Great Spirit.

Love can be the warm feeling in your heart that you experience when dating someone special. It can also be the protective rush you feel when your toddler is about to put a toy into an electrical outlet. Or the passion you feel when you and your partner disagree. It can be the grief that overcomes you when a parent passes away. It can also be the joy of laughing with your best friend. Love is an emotion, but it's also an experience of divine energy that encompasses all of those emotions. Love is All.

It's helpful to form a more concrete connection to love when you're in a dark time. Visualize it as a bright light shining right over your head. Hear it as your favorite song. Smell it as a rose. Touch it as a plush stuffed animal, your pet's soft fur, or your baby's cheek. Taste it as a decadent dessert. What sensations pull you into your heart? Find them because it's there that you'll experience love.

Think of your heart chakra as one big container. Let divine energy fill that container and then pour out through your whole being. Love is presence. Love is power. Love is the power of real magic.

Take a deep breath. Bring all your awareness into your heart. Take a few more deep breaths and let love in. Let in the presence of the Divine.

Blessed Be.

Forgiveness Restores Your Power

Pain and trauma need healing. When you're hurt in some way, you need to restore a feeling of safety and power. Healing occurs by loving the part of you that has been disoriented, bewildered, and scared. It starts with having tender compassion for yourself and an acceptance of your life as it is in the present moment. Feel your feelings, and listen to the sad, insecure, or scared part of yourself in just the same kindly way you'd listen to an adorable five-year-old child, i.e.without judgment. Don't rush the process. Stay in the grief, anger, or sadness until you've exhausted those emotions. Then, let love in.

Healing can also mean truly forgiving the person who hurt you. That doesn't mean you condone their behaviour or spiritually bypass the painful emotions it caused. Forgiveness allows you to release the energy of resentment from your body and open that space for something that feels better, like peace or joy.

We have a responsibility to love one another. When we're in integrity, it feels awful to harm another person or the earth. When someone intentionally hurts you, they are breaking a sacred code. Moral harm requires spiritual repair. Sometimes, it is beyond us to love and forgive. Sometimes, it has to happen in a moment of divine intervention, when we're flooded with grace.

All is love. This statement is a foundational principle of many sacred texts, including *A Course in Miracles,* a book by Helen Schucman. The concept of "All" includes even those painful experiences, forces of destruction, or people who hurt us. If we see those things or people as our enemies, we establish a polarity within ourselves, an unhealthy imbalance. It then requires a lot of our energy to hold onto our resentment or anger. And it doesn't feel good in our bodies. Energy wants to move and flow, like water. If it stagnates, it can become toxic to our systems.

Forgiveness can move stagnant energy and free us to feel more powerful in our lives. Forgiveness is also a process; it doesn't mean we don't feel sadness, anger, or rage. It means when we feel these emotions, we also find ways to move them through and out of our bodies. Give them to the earth or your divine helpers; they know how to transmute them. Dance, sing, punch, kick, or run out those emotions. Just move them through and out of your body.

Our Deepest Fear Is Our Power

The brightest light in us is power and so is the darkest dark. We're afraid of our potentiality—our creative power to build or destroy. We have within us the capacity to harm others in big ways. To kill. To abuse. To sever ties. To commit suicide. To take advantage of one another. We fear that voice inside that says, "I wish he were dead!" Or "I could just hit her!" We fear being the "bad" guy or girl because we learned that bad boys and girls get in trouble. And so, we fear our own darkness. We suppress our anger and rage. We would rather become a victim of circumstances than a perpetrator of violence.

But our emotions want to flow, including anger and rage. Alchemically, water is connected to our feelings and so we can draw on that metaphor when thinking about how to manage such intense emotions. Water that stagnates becomes toxic. Bacteria and parasites propagate quickly in still waters. Water is meant to meander and flow. When we judge or resist our emotions, they stagnate too and can then become harmful to us or others. If we deny our joy, we can become bitter. If we deny anger, we can invite depression. If we deny grief, we can breed apathy.

When we resist anything, we give it attention; we feed it with our magical power. Those dark thoughts and intense feelings want your awareness, but you want to move them along. Obsession can lead to stagnation. When you have dark thoughts or feelings, acknowledge and accept them. Then, transmute them.

Our darkness does not intend to harm. It is a wildfire, inspiring, purifying, and enlivening us. It is a rage that cries out against injustices or pushes us to advocate for a cause. It is our passion, depth, and intensity. If you want to activate your light, you have to accept and *trust* your dark. Your darkness wants only to be honored as a part of the whole. When you're whole, you're in integrity. And when you're in integrity, you would cringe to do harm. You're not a vibrational match to violence or wrongdoing.

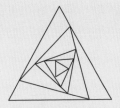

Embracing Your Dark Side

1. Center yourself, drawing your awareness to your heart center. Let love swell in your heart as you focus on the tender core of you.

2. Say to your dark side, "I invite you to come out and play. Come out of the shadows. Let's talk." Wait for its response.

3. Ask your dark side what it most needs. Ask how you can honor it while also honoring your light.

4. Ask your dark side for a face or image to symbolize it. Draw that image if you feel inspired.

5. Start a conversation with your dark side. Journal some of this dialog if it feels in the flow to do so.

6. When you feel complete, thank your dark side, thank your light side, and close the circle (see pages 180–181).

Creation and Destruction

As an astrologer, I'm highly attuned to the universe's cyclical nature and nature's perfectly- orchestrated timing. The seasons of the year reflect this. We see buds bursting open in the springtime as new life abounds. Then, in the summer, we have an abundance of light to nurture spring's new life. In the autumn, we reap the harvest and save our yield for the winter, the time when seedpods and leaves fall, and nature goes to sleep.

In our lives, too, we have seasons for new beginnings and creation and seasons for endings and destruction. Seasons of endings can feel like dark times. They can feel chaotic in the truest sense of the word.

Creative and Destructive Cycles

To the ancient Greeks, *chaos* was the state of dark emptiness, the void preceding the creation of the universe. When I think of *chaos* in this context, I imagine millions of subatomic particles all flying around, looking for their counterparts and trying to arrange themselves, like sperm swimming frantically toward an egg—restless, hurried, and excited. Our consciousness directs those subatomic particles into form, and things manifest in our lives. The energy of chaos is intense!

It's dynamic, wild, and unsettled. Out of chaos, ideas emerge:

I'm going to move.
I want to have a baby.
I'm ready to fall in love.
Once upon a time …
Hey! I could make money doing this thing I love.
I'd like to meet new friends and build community.
I need help.

I like to think there are angels of creation and angels of destruction, which motivate new beginnings and endings. Sometimes those angels of destruction come in the form of a lover who decides to leave the relationship. Sometimes, they come in the form of a flood or house fire. They could present themselves as a global pandemic, war, or illness. Angels of destruction could come in the form of a missed opportunity. When angels of destruction come into our lives, we say: "How could this be happening?" We feel grief. We're frustrated by our seeming lack of power. In these times, the angels of creation surround us, whisper ideas into our minds, and guide us through the chaos.

Creative cycles often start in the dark, after we've experienced loss or hardship, or after we've felt stuck and confused. That's when we decide to make a change. Then, the creative cycle escalates, and we blossom, feeling alive with possibility. The excitement is palpable. We take careful steps to nurture our intentions. The energy of excitement and enthusiasm fuels our courage and motivates us to take the next steps forward.

Destructive cycles illuminate what needs to change in our lives. We might say goodbye to a person, leave a job, or have to move home. Being in the midst of an ending can feel painful. We experience grief, sadness, or disappointment. Yet, things need to die for others to be born.

We cannot rush destructive cycles, no matter how awful they feel. By going into the darkness and feeling those intense emotions, we generate precious energy—magic—to shape our lives anew.

Journal Prompt

WHERE DO I FEEL STAGNANT ENERGY IN MY BODY?

WHAT EMOTIONS ARE STUCK THERE?

WHAT IS MY BODY TELLING ME I NEED TO FORGIVE?

HOW CAN I FORGIVE?

WHAT DOES MY BODY WANT OR NEED FROM ME TO MOVE THIS ENERGY OUT?

AFTER YOU'VE FINISHED, HONOR YOUR BODY'S NEEDS AND MOVE
IT IN WHATEVER WAYS IT WANTS TO MOVE.

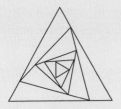

MAGICAL EXERCISE:

Transmuting Emotions

1. Feel an emotion you'd like to transmute. What words describe the feeling?

sour	nauseous	tight
hot	pouty	dangerous
sweet	itchy	tense
cold	weak	sensitive
milky	mean	bitter
furrowed	red	painful
hard	dry	wet
closed	heavy	sharp
white	soft	salty
angry	spasm	achy
tender	black	

2. Where do you feel this emotion in your body? Place your hand on that space and send love through your hand. Imagine it flowing from a white light at your head through your arm and out your palm.

3. Visualize this emotion as a little white ball and your body as a great labyrinth. Now, you're going to have to move for this one! Ask your body where it wants to move in order to release this little ball of energy. Wiggle that ball through your body until you are ready to release it through your hands or feet. Once it is out of your body, visualize it dissolving into the earth.

Magic Rule #5 :

Be
Whole

8

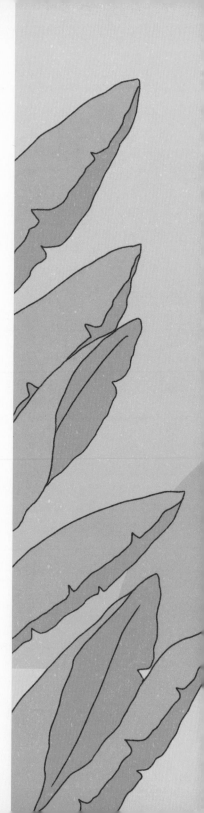

Each one of us is a universe unto ourselves. We are all complex and multifaceted. We are light, dark, spirit, and body, all wrapped into one whole. And when we integrate the different facets of ourselves, we will find we have more energy—more power—to focus on our magical acts.

Integration means being in integrity. It means your words align with your actions, your thoughts align with your deeds, and your Ego Self agrees with your Higher Self, even when it's inconvenient.

In this chapter, we learn a process of integration to bring your whole self into alignment. Not only will you feel more powerful in your life and more at home in your body, you'll also amaze yourself with the effectiveness and power of your magical acts. This chapter is hands-on and experiential. So, I invite you to now enter into your journey of self-discovery.

Daily Practice

Take five deep breaths. Press your palms together at your heart center and press your legs and feet together. Visualize a line of light moving through the center of your body from head to foot. Then, relax, shaking out your hands and arms.

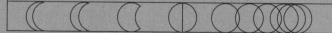

Integrating Spirit and Body

It's no secret; many of us want to practice magic to manifest some of our deep desires. Yet, we don't always get what we want after doing rituals and spells. Why is that?

1. Your Divine Self has other plans.
2. It's not aligned with the other people involved, or with nature.
3. You're not fully integrated into that desire. Parts of you don't want it.

Working with magic doesn't always mean you will manifest what you want when you want it. It means being in your body on this planet at this moment as a conduit for divine energy. From the meeting point of presence and connection, you can shift consciousness. And it feels truly magical to see evidence of a shift through synchronicities, signs, and wonders.

If your Higher Self wants the experience of fulfilling your intention, it will find a way. If not, your desire for that intention to manifest will lead you to some other purpose. For this reason, it's important to integrate your spirit with your body. Your body is your guide in communicating with your spirit.

Your Body Is a Divination Tool

Your body is your No. 1 divination tool. It gives clear signals when anything's out of alignment, or a part of you is off-line. It's also your guide for when someone is deceiving you, or something is unsafe.

Do you remember the **Body Awareness Exercise** from Chapter 2 (see page 43). I recommend trying that as often as possible to fine-tune your perception of body signals. Get to know your inner *yes, no,* and *maybe.* The more body awareness you have, the better you'll be able to access your intuition and work with magic. When something's out of alignment, you'll feel it in your bones, heart, gut, or somewhere else in your body.

When we judge any aspect of our body, we limit our experience of spirit. You may see things you'd like to improve but labeling those as "bad" without a more in-depth inquiry denies you the opportunity to see the symbolism and meaning those body parts are offering.

For example, my Grandmother loved the art of Chinese face reading; she taught me that the two lines between my eyebrows relate to the liver. I dug deeper and discovered a correlation between the liver and anger. And so, I decided to change my relationship with anger and see if it made a difference. I had always been afraid of expressing my anger, and those two lines were evidence of its suppression. So, I bought a punching bag and set aside time each week to feel that anger and move it through my body. Now, several years later, those lines are no longer as prominent as they were back then.

When our bodies are in pain, or we're suffering from an illness, a deeper inquiry might be the last thing we want. Chronic conditions or past trauma can lead us to feel a separation between body and spirit. Your body might feel like an ill-fitting costume, or you may want to disassociate from it altogether. When your body expresses discomfort, your spirit cries for attention. Use your body as a divination tool.

Think of each body part as being like a tarot card with layers of symbolism and meaning. To integrate body and spirit, learn to unpack the layers. Books like *You Can Heal Your Life* by Louise Hay can help you decipher meaning from physical ailments and conditions. A good dream dictionary will also help you identify the symbolism for most body parts.

When we investigate the messages that our bodies are giving us, we help to integrate our bodies and spirits. The more integrated we are, the more we trust ourselves (Magic Rule #1). So, love your body—even the parts that feel most unlovable to you.

Integration

Imagine a bright white light that flows from the heavens above down through your chakras and on down through you and out into the earth. The point of integration is that line of light. When we're out of sync, we feel it—physically, mentally, and spiritually. But we cannot be in integrity until we unite the invisible divine and the visible earth.

SPIRIT

Divine Self
Higher Self

With

BODY

Ego Self
Subconscious Self

LIGHT

Visible, conscious, what's seen,
how we identify ourselves

With

DARK

Subconscious, hidden,
what's not known,
what's in the shadows

SELF

Mind, body, spirit

With

OTHER

Spirit guides and divine helpers,
the cosmos, people, creatures,
the earth

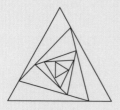

Body Awareness Two

1. To begin, let's revisit your primary intention. Write it down again to give it your energy. Embody your intention by moving it through each of your chakras.

2. Now, draw your awareness to the crown of your head. State your intention aloud or in your mind. Notice what physical sensations you feel. (You may notice thoughts as well, but for now, focus on what's happening in your body.) What tingling, pulsing, or tightening sensations do you feel? Each feeling also offers clues about whether you're in alignment with your intention.

3. Move your awareness into the middle of your forehead to your third-eye chakra. State your intention aloud or in your mind. Notice the physical sensations you now feel.

4. Move your awareness into your throat. State your intention aloud or in your mind. Notice the physical sensations you feel.

5. Move your awareness to your chest—your heart center. State your intention aloud or in your mind. Notice what physical sensations you feel.

6. Shift your awareness to your solar plexus. State your intention aloud or in your mind. Notice what physical sensations you feel.

7.   Shift your awareness to your navel and focus about two inches below it. State your intention aloud or in your mind. Notice what physical sensations you feel.

8.   Move your awareness to your root chakra, the point between the base of your spine and pubic bone. State your intention aloud or in your mind. Notice what physical sensations you feel.

9.   What signals did your body give you about your openness or resistance to the manifestation of your intention? Write them down in your journal.

Your Body's Signals

Thinking about the exercise you've just completed, here are some clues about the messages your body might be sending. (Of course, if you have persistent pain or ailments that don't go away, please seek medical help.)

CROWN CHAKRA

If you felt tingling at your crown like electrical currents moving through you, then perhaps your intention has been inspired. Your Higher Self and Divine Self are in resonance. If you felt tightness in your body, especially around your head, try phrasing your intention in a different way. Is it too detailed? Too vague?

THIRD-EYE CHAKRA

If you felt tingling around your forehead, you can envision your intention coming to fruition and discern the next steps to take. If you felt tense or were distracted, you may doubt yourself. Or you could be afraid to see something. Take a deep breath and ask yourself what you can't see.

THROAT CHAKRA

If you felt tingling in your throat area, say your intention aloud with vigor! Let it ring through your vocal cords. You are ready to own your intention and take the next steps forward. If you felt tightness, numbness, or tension in your neck or shoulders, ask yourself why you're afraid of stating your intention. Which part of you is resistant to the fulfillment of your desire?

HEART CHAKRA

If you felt a warm fullness like an overflowing of gratitude and love in your heart center, you can feel the fulfillment of your intention. You are full of magic. If you felt disconnected from your heart, spaced out, or tense in your chest or back, send love into that space and try again. Make your heart center a space to welcome your intention. Often, intentions won't settle into our hearts if we don't feel deserving of goodness. Love is the remedy for that.

SOLAR PLEXUS CHAKRA

If you felt a sense of strength and certainty in your solar plexus, you own your intention and you're ready for it to manifest. If you felt tightness, shortness of breath, anxiety, or sadness, fear or shame may be preventing you from feeling powerful. Ask yourself: To whom or what am I giving my power? How can I claim it back?

SACRAL CHAKRA

If you felt warmth, tingling like electricity, or excitement in your navel center, then you're in a creative process. The seeds have been planted and nurtured. Wait for them to bear fruit. If you felt any tension, soreness in your back, digestive distress, or bloating, ask yourself: What part of me is afraid of my magical power? What part of me doesn't want my intention to reach fullness?

ROOT CHAKRA

If you felt openness, warmth, or tingling in your root chakra, then you are grounded in your desires and ready to embody your magic. Integration will still help. If you held your breath, felt discomfort in your lower body, or grew tired, then some aspect of you doesn't feel it's entirely safe to bring your intention to fruition. Ask yourself: Is the fulfillment of my intention for my best and highest good? Why or why not?

You can see now that with any signals your body sends, you can ascertain guiding information. Simply ask the questions.

Journal Prompt

WITH YOUR EYES CLOSED, SCAN YOUR BODY FROM HEAD TO TOE. NOTICE ANY SENSATIONS THAT DRAW YOUR ATTENTION. CHOOSE THE ONE THAT FEELS THE MOST INTENSE FOR THIS EXERCISE. FIRST, RELAX BY TIGHTENING AND RELEASING THE MUSCLES AROUND THAT PART OF YOUR BODY. THEN, ASK YOUR BODY THE FOLLOWING QUESTIONS:

WHAT ARE YOU TRYING TO TELL ME?

HOW CAN I HELP YOU?

WHAT CAN YOU TELL ME ABOUT MY POWER?

WHAT ELSE DO I NEED TO KNOW?

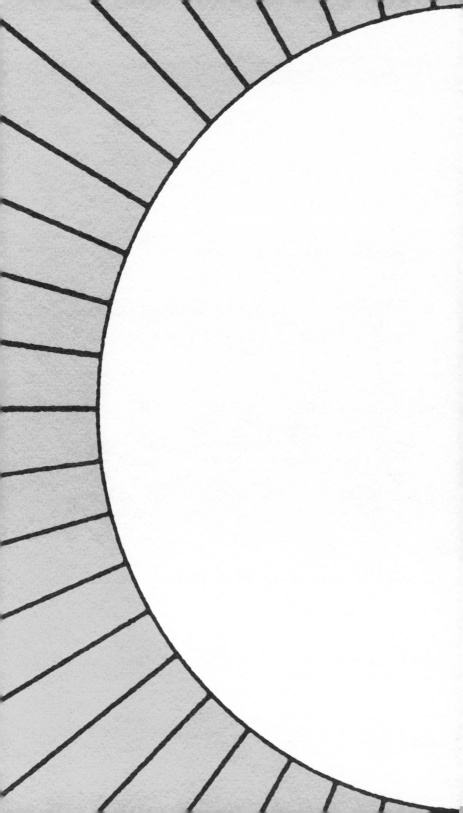

Magic Is Erotic

Magical energy is a creative, life-force energy. It's an erotic power—which means we sense, feel, and experience it in our bodies. It enlivens every cell, including the pleasure centers in our bodies. Sometimes, we may feel it as a yearning. Sometimes, it's the passionate energy we sense when we're making love. Sex can be a way of generating energy to focus toward an intention because, in these heightened states of pleasure, our Ego Self takes a rest. So, sex can be a transcendent experience that raises our vibration enough to allow us to access higher states of consciousness. In those times, we let go of resistance or fear and can better allow the free flow of magical power.

To the philosopher Plato, eros is a spiritual form of love that motivates us toward transformation and union with the Divine. In his book *The Symposium,* the character Diotima of Mantinea, a prophetess and wise woman, describes *eros* to Socrates as a spiritual force that serves as an intermediary between humans and the Divine. When we work with magic, we draw on this type of energy. However, it doesn't have to be limited to physical sexual acts. In her 1978 essay, *Uses of the Erotic: The Erotic as Power,* Audre Lorde describes erotic power as a dimension of personal power that intersects spirituality, feeling, and sexuality. She describes this power as a deeply feminine and spiritual power rooted in "nonrational knowledge." When you work with magic, you open yourself to experiencing the erotic as power.

Pleasure is our right. It makes our body a welcome place for our spirits to inhabit. It reinforces a sense of safety. Have you ever wondered if part of your purpose in life is just to experience the joys of being in a physical body? The experience of tasting delicious food motivates us to eat. Sexual pleasure drives us to reproduce. All sensual pleasures—sight, sound, smell, taste, and touch—also serve the purpose of protecting us from danger and keeping us safe and alive.

However, we can cross signals. If we learn pleasure is sinful or wrong, for example, we might feel ashamed for wanting what we want. If you inherit beliefs which assert that sexual desire is sinful, or if early experiences of sexual trauma marry pleasure with shame, magic can be a force for transformation and healing. Magic can help dissolve that shame and integrate your spirit and body.

Shame left in the shadows becomes toxic, and shrouds pleasure in a cloak of judgment. When pleasure and shame come together, we need help to disconnect the two. We need to love our whole selves.

As a child, I heard my mom and aunts say, "A moment on your lips, a lifetime on your hips," when we passed the desserts around the dinner table. Consequently, I learned to feel guilty each time I ate a piece of chocolate cake or other sweet treats. Guilt and shame can add such toxicity to pleasure.

Being in integrity—integrated—allows us to check in with ourselves and ask, "Is this what I *really* want?" Be willing to hear the answer and be open to that answer changing from time to time. Some days, indulging might be just what your body wants, and it might serve your highest good. When we judge our desires, we simply reinforce that separation between the body and the spirit.

So now, when you have a craving or physical desire, ask questions and find out more about it. Center your awareness in your heart and ask your body, "Is this for my highest good?" You can do this with every decision you make. Use the **Body Awareness Exercise** in Chapter 2 (see page 43) to find the answer.

What Are You Craving?

Curiosity keeps us from judging. When we have cravings, rather than resort to restriction or indulgence, we can decide to decipher these clues to our deeper needs by exploring the symbolism of those desires. For example, did you know that specific astrological cycles enhance our sense of physical pleasure and our desire for sensual experiences? When the moon is in Taurus, we might crave sweet foods. When it is in Cancer, we tend to have a bigger appetite and crave comfort food.

In addition to the daily astrological cycles that we all experience together, your personal astrological transits can indicate times when you have more self-discipline and are more inclined to turn down the chocolate cake.

Each food type has an astrological correspondence and alchemical purpose. And no food is inherently *bad*. When you have a craving, ask yourself what it might mean symbolically. When you crave a type of food or indulgent activity, look at the astrological correspondence and see if you're craving something emotional or spiritual as well. Then you can meet the deeper needs if you wish to resist the physical urge. Here are some examples:

Sun and Leo
CRAVING: Sunshine, citrus fruit, rice, foods rich in magnesium, Vitamins A and D
SYMBOLIC MEANING: Self-confidence, creativity, playfulness

Moon and Cancer
CRAVING: Comfort food and emotional eating, vegetables, water, shellfish, chicken, seaweed, dairy, foods rich in potassium
SYMBOLIC MEANING: Emotions, fertility, nurturing

Mercury and Gemini or Virgo
CRAVING: Fasting, exercise, grains, wheat, poultry, foods rich in thiamine (Vitamin B1
SYMBOLIC MEANING: Detoxification, communication, mental activities

Venus and Taurus or Libra

CRAVING: Creature comforts, shopping, indulgence, carbohydrates, sugar, candy, fruit, beans, potatoes, foods rich in Vitamin E, copper, and niacin
SYMBOLIC MEANING: Beauty, relationships, balance, financial stability, pleasure

Mars and Aries

CRAVING: Exercise, sex, proteins, amino acids, foods rich in iron or Vitamin B12
SYMBOLIC MEANING: Vitality, strength, boundaries, protection, autonomy

Jupiter and Sagittarius

CRAVINGS: Excess and indulgence, fats, cholesterol, foods rich in Vitamin K and biotin (Vitamin B7)
SYMBOLIC MEANING: Faith, optimism, generosity, adventure, knowledge

Saturn and Capricorn

CRAVINGS: Pleasure restriction, salt, protein, barley, foods rich in Vitamin C, folic acid, and calcium
SYMBOLIC MEANING: Structure, rules, tradition, history, ambition

Uranus and Aquarius

CRAVING: Abstinence from food, foods rich in zinc
SYMBOLIC MEANING: Community, individuality, future visions, innovation

Neptune and Pisces

CRAVING: Alcohol, caffeine, nicotine, drugs, food additives, seaweed, fish
SYMBOLIC MEANING: Mysticism, dreams, creativity, escapism

Pluto and Scorpio

CRAVING: Sex, enzymes, bacteria, fermented foods
SYMBOLIC MEANING: Healing, rebirth, power, psychological exploration

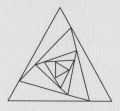

MAGICAL EXERCISE:

Bringing Body and Spirit Together

1. Stand or sit upright.

2. Hold your arms up towards the sky.

3. Picture your body as one big triangle. Invite divine energy from the top of your fingertips to the bottom of your feet.

4. Plant your feet into the ground. Draw energy up from the earth through your feet and out through your fingertips.

    Say:

    I integrate body and spirit.
    I am invisible divine, and visible human, as one.
    I purify myself of all shame.
    My body is a conduit of love.
    I embody it and share it with others and the natural world.
    And so it is.

ONE QUICK NOTE

While we've talked about honoring pleasure and our desires, it's important to note our integrated selves would not agree to experiencing satisfaction at the expense of another person. True integration allows you to be hypersensitive to the energies of the world around you. When you're integrated, your heightened intuition enables you to feel others' emotions. You develop deep empathy and compassion. Your integrated self is not a vibrational match to deception, either by lying to yourself or betraying another person.

If you have desires that could be harmful to another person or yourself, please seek therapeutic help or support. You don't have to manage those feelings alone. We can experience pleasure but not act in a way that compromises our integrity. And just because we feel something doesn't mean we have to act on it!

Intergrating
Dark and Light

Desire is born within both our dark side (the hidden aspects of our unconscious self) and our light side (the conscious part of us). Desire alone, and not only fulfilling that desire, can lead us to growth and spiritual transformation. Let me say that again in a different way. Don't judge what you want. Wants are like stepping-stones on life's path. When we take a step towards what we want, we may arrive at that destination, (yay!) or we may never arrive at that destination, but in taking that step towards or away from what we want, arrive at an even more fulfilling end.

In childhood, we learn what's acceptable or unacceptable to our early caregivers. Because attention equals power, we feel a stronger sense of our potentiality when we receive attention for certain behaviors. Rewards and praise for good grades let us know our intelligence is a resource of power. If fellow students laugh at your jokes in class, your humor becomes a resource of power. Over time, you test out different ways of attracting attention, and this translates into feeling loved. But we also learn what behaviors make us feel unloved. Our Ego Selves feed on this reinforcement, and they structure beliefs and fears accordingly.

As a result, we limit ourselves to a specific set of skills, interests, behaviors, and emotions that fall within the range of what we have learned to be "acceptable". Over time, we learn to shape our identities around those skills, interests, behaviors, and emotions. Our potentiality involves those natural inclinations, but it also includes skills, interests, behaviors, and emotions that fall outside of the range of what's acceptable or praised. When we avoid what isn't familiar or comfortable, we may strive to reach our potential, but we can never really feel truly fulfilled.

Our potential is more than we can ever imagine because our souls are pure infinite potential. Our Ego, Higher, and Subconscious Selves are the organizing principles for that pure potential. So, the next time you think, "I'm not living up to my potential," know that you're right. Then, give yourself a break!

Magic invites you to see yourself as a whole. To do this, try new things and stretch yourself beyond your comfort zone. Remember the dualism we talked about in the last chapter? When you see yourself as good at one thing and bad at another, you're in duality. Instead, see your potential to be both/and. Both mathematical and artistic. Both emotional and logical. Both smart and funny. Both a people-pleaser and a narcissist.

Often the people in our lives who trigger the most intense emotions reflect to us what might be hidden in ourselves. If you find yourself being annoyed, frustrated, angry, attracted, or intrigued by someone, ask yourself what are the aspects of that person you can't see in yourself. Be willing to see everything, and you will then be able to give attention (and love) to your whole self.

Our personalities are an integral part of our Ego Self. The archetypes with which we identify are in the light of our conscious awareness, while those with which we don't are in our dark hidden unconscious. But our hidden aspects have as much, if not more, power than the conscious parts of ourselves. And those aspects of you that you've relegated to the shadows tend to attract circumstances into your life to help you bring them into the light.

As we discussed in Chapter 4, the different parts of us can want different things at different times. Integrating our Ego and Subconscious Selves can feel like herding cats! These hidden aspects of ourselves are sensed and felt. It can be challenging to bring them into conscious awareness because, well, they're in the dark. When you integrate the visible with the hidden, you become so much more powerful. Do not be afraid to see everything—see all of yourself.

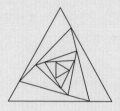

MAGICAL EXERCISE:

Integration

Go back to the archetypes list printed on page 65. Look again at this list and choose four with which you strongly identify. Also choose four that feel nothing like you.

1. About the four with which you most identify, answer the following questions:

When was the first time I felt a resonance with this identity?

How was that persona positively reinforced in my life?

In what ways does my identification with this identity limit me?

In what way does it benefit me?

2. About the four with which you least identify, answer the following questions:

In my life, which person or group of people most reflect this identity back to me?

What about that person or people most triggers or intrigues me?

Is there any part of me that wants to become more like this?

How would my life change if I were to accept this identity as a part of my personality?

MEDITATION:

Integration Meditation

1. Take a few deep breaths and relax your body. Visualize a globe of light around your body. In your mind, say: "I am safe and whole."

2. Imagine you're walking on a path and come to a door with glowing light around the edges. The door opens, and you enter to find a staircase.

3. Descend the stairs. When you're at the bottom, you will find four people who represent different aspects of yourself. Allow them to approach you.

4. Ask each one what they are here to teach you? Spend a few moments with each one. Get to know them. As you do, feel the love you have for them grow and feel their gratitude for the connection in return. Take as long as you need.

5. When you finish, visualize hugging those representatives of your Unconscious Self. Then, imagine walking back up the stairs, out the door, and follow the path back to where you started.

6. Journal any observations or feelings you had as you journeyed into your dark side. Anytime you experience a Magic Crisis, you can explore your dark side for clues about what needs to be integrated for you to experience the fullness of your power.

Intergrating
Self and Other

Have you ever thought of someone, and then they call or text? Or have you had an encounter with an animal that you later realized was an omen? Our Divine Self is pure unindividuated consciousness, and it merges with the consciousness of others and nature.

As I'm writing this, I'm aware of a screeching hawk. My awareness invites the hawk's consciousness to merge with mine. What information can I glean from understanding the symbolism of the hawk? While we can't talk, I can still communicate with it by sensing what messages I feel, hear, or see when I become aware of it. When I allow my consciousness to expand beyond my body, I invite messengers into my life.

Think of your "self" as one large globe of energy. While your spirit resides within your physical body, its consciousness extends beyond it. It's united with the consciousness of the whole earth. When we hold tight to our identities and see ourselves as separate from others, we fall into the trap of judgment. And as we've seen, within polarity lies hierarchy, with this separation causing us to see ourselves as greater than or lesser than others. Consequently, we end up in a constant quest for empowerment, by seeking a power that emanates from outside of ourselves. Empowerment is assigned, given, and sometimes taken.

Magical power is different in that it is inherent—it is power from within you. When you integrate yourself and others, you open yourself up to an expanded awareness of self. This shift in consciousness makes it possible for you to communicate with others across time and space; to access intuitive information for loved ones;and magically draw helpful people into your life.

Love is the unifier. Remember this statement from Chapter 7? If all is love; we are all united in love. While you have a body, mind, and spirit that's uniquely "you", you're also part of the consciousness of the whole. Magic pulls you into that enormous consciousness where you can access wisdom and knowledge from beyond your Ego Self's limited scope of understanding.

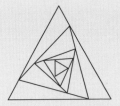

MAGICAL EXERCISE:

Integrate Self and Other

1. Ground and connect with the earth. If you are near a tree, lean against it and feel it supporting you. Press the soles of your feet into the ground below. Say aloud or in your mind, "Earth, we are one."

2. Breathe in the air and let it fill your lungs. What does it feel like in your body? Experience the air as it flows against your face and body. Say, "Sky, we are one."

3. Take a deep breath into your stomach and exhale with a big sigh. Repeat this five times, bringing your awareness into your lower abdomen.

4. Let your mind relax. Imagine a globe of light at your heart center. Visualize that light expanding beyond your body and glowing around your immediate area. Sit still and observe.

5. What pulls your attention? Does the earth want to connect with you? Is a creature making noise? Is the grass itchy? Listen to and feel those connections. Feel your consciousness merge with theirs.

6. Try not to think in words; let your awareness transcend language. Feel yourself becoming one with nature.

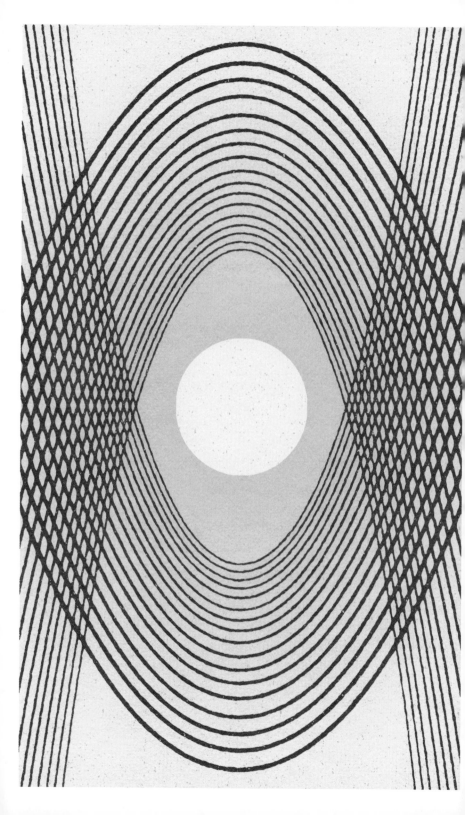

7. If you have difficulty getting out of your head, rest your chin on your chest, close your eyes, and direct your gaze down and to the right. Breathe deeply. The more you relax, the more you let your Ego Self know it's safe to take a break.

You can also do this exercise with another person:

1. Both of you center your awareness in your hearts. Set the intention to merge with them.

2. Now, feel what they're feeling. What do you hear in your mind? What images can you see in your mind's eye? What feelings do you feel in your body?

3. It may take a few minutes to relax into this exercise. Give yourself time. Try gazing into one another's eyes and then letting your vision blur, so the other person shifts out of focus. You may now notice their aura. You may even hear their thoughts. Take it all in without saying a word to them.

4. When you feel complete, stop, draw your awareness into your own body, and shake out your arms and legs. Visualize that globe of light moving back into your heart center.

5. Ground your energy again.

Magic Rule #6 :

Relax and Allow

9

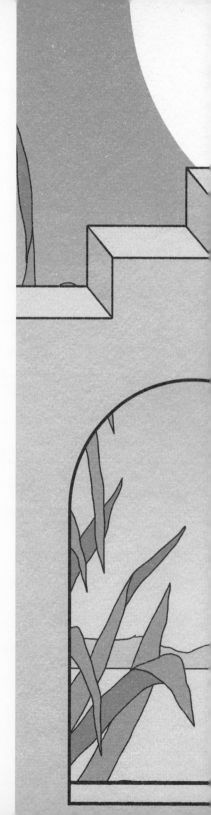

Magic Rule #6 leads us to surrender; and we free-fall into the arms of the Divine. We enter a state of relaxation beyond fear and simply allow magic to happen. In this chapter, you'll learn how to dissolve fear by discovering its root source. You'll then learn ways to let your Ego Self rest as you enter into different states of consciousness where you will feel no resistance to the flow of spiritual energy and your magical power.

As you read this chapter, I encourage you to relax your body and quiet your distracting thoughts. So, pause, pour a cup of tea, light a candle, stream some ambient music, and kick up your feet.

Daily Practice

Establish a rhythm. Feel your heartbeat, and for 10 minutes use your hands to drum a beat similar to your heartbeat—about 60 beats per minute. For this exercise, you can use a drum or the surface of a table.

Surrender

In graduate school, I spent several weeks in Germany researching the witch trials. Not knowing the language or geography, I spent some valuable research time lost and running into dead ends. One day, I realized I'd walked through the same busy intersection for the third time, and my phone's map had been leading me in circles. Asking for directions proved a futile effort with the language barrier. I was lost ... again.

Exasperated, I stopped walking, put my phone away, and raised my hands in surrender. Suddenly, I sensed what could only be the warm flow of magic moving through my body, and I felt immediately calm. A voice inside whispered, "Keep going straight." I looked ahead and saw a path leading to a garden gate covered with ivy. I opened the gate, and to my amazement, I found myself in a botanical garden teeming with life.

Sculptures of gods and goddesses lined the pathway under the covered archway. On either side were vibrant flowers and birdsong melodies. I kept walking, and the path ended on the very street I had been trying to find. I stayed in the park for a while, overcome with awe. The beauty was breathtaking, and I would never have been able to tak it in had I not been willing to let go of my plans and surrender to magic.

I remained in this state of openness throughout my trip. Magic led me into a rose garden dedicated to the burned witches; old castle remains with patches of four-leaf clover; historians and translators who helped me understand the first-person narratives I had found; and much more. My research was about gender, power, and justice, but the discoveries I made about magic planted the seeds for this book that you're working with now.

Journal
Prompt

THINK ABOUT A TIME IN YOUR LIFE WHEN EVERYTHING FELT MAGICAL.
WRITE A SHORT STORY DESCRIBING THAT TIME AS IF YOU'RE WRITING ABOUT
A FICTIONAL CHARACTER.

ONCE UPON A TIME ...

AFTER YOU FINISH WRITING THE STORY, REFLECT ON YOUR CHARACTER'S
EXPERIENCE. WHAT, IF ANYTHING, DID YOUR CHARACTER TEACH YOU
ABOUT RELAXING AND ALLOWING? ABOUT MAGIC?

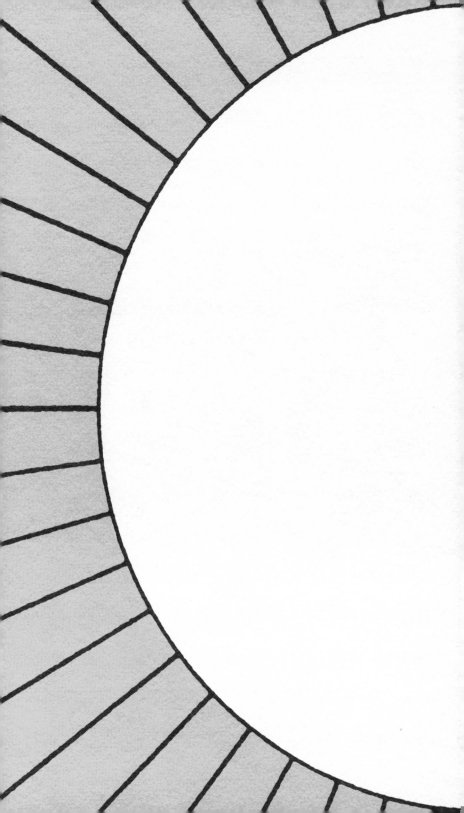

Magic Likes to Flow— Not to Be Controlled

How many times have you wished you could either speed up or slow down the timing of your life? When I work with clients who have unmet desires, they want to know how to fast-track manifestation. "What can I do to make this happen faster?" We are programmed to believe our work and productivity will determine our success in life. Activity is considered more valuable and virtuous than receptivity. Magic wants both; but mostly it wants you to sit still so it can humble you with awe.

Control is not power—not a magical power, that is. Control stems from the Ego Self's drive to be unique or to belong. When we are in a state of surrender and receptivity, divine energy flows to and through us, which means we can access our spiritual gifts of intuition, healing, spirit communication, divination, and more. But fear keeps us from this "surrender-to-the-flow" state.

I want to distinguish here between two different types of fear. The first is the type you experience when you're in immediate danger. It's a rational fear, and one that tells your body to move quickly towards safety. The other is more subtle and insidious, and it arises any time you are about to push against the confines of your comfort zone and grow to new heights and depths. This is the fear of your own power. The roots of it stretch back through our early childhoods and ancestral lines. This fear is karmic and can be unconscious and vague.

We often can't pinpoint its inception point unless we excavate our Subconscious Self through self-reflection, talk therapy, or other healing modalities. We feel this fear physiologically each time we stretch and grow, for, during those times, we often risk rejection, judgment, or the possibility of outgrowing relationships with those we love. This type of fear can manifest itself in several ways, including doubt, obsessive thoughts, worry, bodily tension, or apprehension. Fortunately, there are practical ways to increase relaxation and shift our consciousness beyond fear.

Just Relax

Is it that easy? Don't we wish it were! To feel relaxed, you have to feel safe. If you have a history of trauma or abuse, it could be more difficult for you to feel safe in the world. And even if you haven't had a history of trauma, your ancestors may have. Our DNA holds these memories, and they influence us in subtle ways. When the world feels unsafe, we have a more difficult time allowing ourselves to be still.

Psychiatrist and psychoanalyst Carl Jung first coined the term "collective unconscious" to explain the part of our psyches that holds universal truths, archetypes, primordial thoughts, and beliefs. We're living our individual lives within a shared experience because we're all members of a whole.

As a psychic medium, I work with the subtle energetic threads that link us together each time I help a client. I can access information for others by connecting soul-to-soul. How is this possible? We are connected in ways beyond what we can imagine, and because of this, we can feel the suffering of others we will never even meet.

The world doesn't always feel safe and how can anyone relax in a world full of violence and suffering? Sometimes, just acknowledging we feel unsafe can make a difference in helping us relax. When we recognize and accept our anxiety and fear, we permit ourselves to be present, even when things aren't perfect. We can then make conscious choices to move beyond the fear by adopting a dedicated practice to quiet our mind, still our body, and quell our unconscious fears. Sometimes, trusting our safety takes divine intervention.

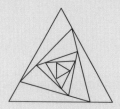

MAGICAL EXERCISE:

Calling Fear into the Light

1. Set a timer for 10 minutes.

2. Rest your chin on your chest, relax your gaze, and take a few deep breaths.

3. Center your awareness in your solar plexus. Invite fear to rise from your core. Don't go looking for it. Let it show itself to you. Sit with it until the timer goes off.

4. After 10 minutes, exhale the fear out of your body. Journal your insights:

    Does your fear have a root cause?
    Where is it centered in your body?
    What color is it?
    What does it have to say?
    What does it need from you?

    When we can personify our fear and have a dialog with it, then we can diffuse its power in our lives.

Presence Is Safety

I feel safest in my body in the world when I'm present, which means I feel my emotions, am attuned to my bodily sensations, am aware of my thoughts, and sense my immediate surroundings. When we bring all of our awareness into the present moment, we can sense that countless possibilities exist right here and now.

We can choose to open our hearts to divine guidance. Then, possibilities we've never considered appear as options for us. When I am present, I can trust the wisdom inherent within my body and drawn from my Higher Self, encouraging me to make choices in support of my highest good.

Bring your awareness into your root chakra, the energy center located in the pelvic floor near the base of your spine. Look around you and notice how safe you feel in your space. What comforts are there for you? What are you enjoying? Presence, beauty, and pleasure can restore our sense of safety even after we've experienced hardship, trauma, and pain.

MAGICAL EXERCISE:

Relax When You're Stressed

STEP ONE: SHAKE IT OFF
Stand and shake your body. Imagine particles of energetic debris falling away from you as you do. Make noise as you shake it all off.

STEP TWO: WORK IT OUT
Run on the spot for several minutes, as fast as you can.

STEP THREE: FEEL YOUR HEARTBEAT
Bring your hands to your chest and feel your heartbeat. Take deep breaths and rest your chin on your chest. As you inhale, say: "I am safe." As you exhale, say: "In my body." Repeat this for five breaths. Then inhale and say, "I am relaxed." Exhale and say, "In my body." Repeat this for five breaths.

Change Your State of Consciousness

In group rituals, you'll often see people dance around fires, beat drums, chant, and sing. These types of practices stir up erotic energy, and this type of physical passion helps transmute fear. The good news is you can also do these activities on your own. (In Chapter 10, we'll discuss how to use these practices in a ritual context.) When we engage in these practices, our brain waves shift into different frequencies, allowing us to relax more deeply. There are several ways you can shift your brain state and enter a heightened state of consciousness:

1. Laughter   **4.** Dancing   **7.** Breathwork

2. Meditation   **5.** Chanting   **8.** Art

3. Drumming   **6.** Playing music

Any time you engage in an activity that allows you to feel timeless, spaceless, and ego-less, you have entered a higher state of consciousness and will be more immune to fear. The above list is by no means exhaustive so you may find other ways to deepen your state of relaxation.

Feeling good and relaxing takes practice. We become used to a range of emotions that serves as a baseline for our daily experiences. So, if you want to feel more relaxed, set the intention and then schedule a daily relaxation practice time.

You may read this and think, "I've struggled with anxiety for so long, there's no way this is going to work for me." Anxiety and depression can be debilitating for many people, and in some cases, medicine can help, in addition to daily spiritual practices. Please seek help from a professional if your life feels unmanageable due to anxiety or depression.

I struggled with anxiety and depression for years, and I couldn't imagine my life any other way. But when I started spiritual development classes, I learned how our thoughts and emotions are like radio frequencies broadcast through our auric fields. My baseline frequency often fell into the range of sadness. I decided I would experiment with raising it and see what differences I experienced in my life.

I dedicated myself to this practice as if I were training for a marathon. Each time I started to feel depressed or anxious, I set a timer for five minutes and flooded my mind with positive thoughts and affirmations that picked me up but still felt true. I told myself things like:

I am willing to feel better at this moment.
I receive abundant blessings from the universe.
I allow more goodness into my life.
I'm grateful for my spiritual guides and helpers.
I am love. I am loved.

This exercise made me much more aware of the relationship between my "self-talk" and my feelings of depression. I wore a rubber band around my wrist as a reminder to shift gears when my thoughts became negative or self-defeating. Within a short time, I started seeing a difference. I met new friends who were so supportive and positive. I became more focused on my goals and less remorseful of the past. My life slowly changed for the better.

The above practices are vehicles to help you arrive at a higher vibration and shift your consciousness. After enough practice, your baseline will change, allowing you to experience more satisfaction and joy.

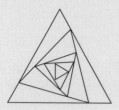

MAGICAL EXERCISE:

Focus Your Energy

1. Engage in one of the previous practices for 20 minutes. Then, think of your primary intention.

2. Close your eyes and see the fulfillment of your primary intention in your third-eye chakra.

3. Send all of the energy you generated to your third-eye chakra and direct it toward your vision.

4. Hold it there for several minutes and then exhale, letting go of any excess energy.

NOTE ABOUT OTHER VIBRATION-RAISING PRACTICES:

There are many ways to raise your vibration in addition to the ones I've listed. Sex is one of them, but only within a safe and consensual context. It may feel safest to do this practice by yourself. If you feel shame or guilt about sexual pleasure, then work through those feelings before relying on this as a relaxation exercise.

Plant medicine can also help some people achieve an enlightened state, but some of it is illegal in parts of the world. If you plan to explore this practice, do it with integrity. Work with an experienced shaman, therapist, or guide. Plan for plenty of integration time after the experience. If you wish to try this, do your research to ensure you stay healthy and safe.

You can arrive at higher states of consciousness without mind-altering substances, and I recommend working with those techniques first.

How Do I Know If It's Fear or Intuition?

When you work with magic, you heighten your senses and deepen your intuition. As you develop these gifts, you might start to receive intuitive impressions about what we might consider "bad news." There's a big difference between these intuitive impressions and fearful imaginings. That difference lies in how you experience them in your body.

To differentiate between fear and intuition, let your body guide you. Intuition speaks to us through body sensations, or a "knowing" that you feel deep in your core. Sometimes, you hear it in your mind like a whisper. It can come as a feeling in your heart or solar plexus. Intuition is often subtle and quiet. It's a gentle nudge from within that says, "Hey, pay attention."

Sometimes, your intuition signals with a body sensation like a muscle cramp or nervous stomach. These messages are often grounded in the body, and while they might trigger us to remain alert, we can be aware without being afraid.

On the other hand, fear is a loud, clamoring voice in your head that can speed up your heart rate and make your imagination go wild. When your intuition signals an alert, but you don't have a context for it, your natural inclination will be to look for clues about what that could be. It's in the gathering of these clues we can imagine the worst. If your thoughts start racing or begin telling you a story, bring yourself back into your body.

It's important to stay calm and relaxed when intuitive insights arise because fear limits our ability to see clearly. Staying relaxed helps you determine the next steps to take. Life is never going to give you more than you can handle. It will all be okay. The next time you feel an overwhelming sense of anxiety, take a deep breath, rest your chin on your chest, and take the time to quiet your mind.

In my early psychic development studies, I learned the importance of our endocrine glands for transmitting spiritual information. The thymus gland, in particular, is a helpful conduit between our body and Higher Self. Your thymus resides behind your breastbone in your chest. If you press on your upper chest, about two inches below your collarbone, you can feel sensitive spots. Tapping on these awakens your thymus gland. Try it now. Gently tap your upper chest with your palm.

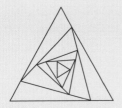

MAGICAL EXERCISE:

Listening to Your Intuition

1. With your chin on your chest, breathe deeply. Have your writing journal ready to go. Listen for the whisper that is your intuition.

    What does your intuition have to say about your primary intention?

    What does your intuition want you to know?

    If you feel a sensation in your body—if a muscle twitches or you feel tense—ask your intuition what it's trying to say through that sense?

    How does your intuition want to differentiate itself from fear?

2. Wait for the responses. You may see something, feel something, or even hear words. Write down any insights or draw pictures of what you see in your mind's eye.

Magic Rule #7:

Ritualize It

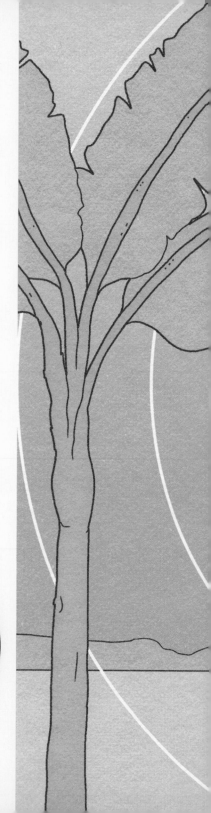

10

A ritual is a performance we give to the unseen forces of magic which brings an idea from the nonphysical realm into the physical one. You can make anything a ritual—taking a shower, brushing your teeth, cooking a meal, or dancing around a fire at the full moon. There is no right way or wrong way to perform a ritual; magic doesn't judge because it knows your intentions—both the ones you state out loud and the ones unspoken in your heart. In this chapter, we discuss different rituals and ritual components, and then we'll try some together.

Daily Practice

Make a ritual out of an everyday task, like taking a shower or cooking a meal.

What changes about that activity?

Notice any changes in your life as you bring sacredness to the mundane.

Ritual Magic

Growing up as a Catholic, I acquired an appreciation for ritual. Every aspect of the Catholic mass has layers of symbolic meaning, and many of them originate from pagan traditions.

I love how rituals give us a framework within which to focus our magical work. We can find comfort in knowing we're in a protective circle and solace too, knowing there's a format to follow. Just like an actor relies on a script and props, so will you have words to speak and symbols to incorporate that help express the desires in your heart.

We all live busy lives. Maybe you're a parent, a professional with a side hustle, or an ambitious person with a demanding job. How can you make time to plan a ritual when you barely have time to eat lunch? The good news is you can make any everyday activity a ritual.

In the morning, my shower is a clearing ritual during which I wash away any distracting or negative thoughts. My breakfast is a gratitude ritual, and I offer thanks to the farmers who helped grow and source the food I eat. Then, I open a circle before starting work. I send love and blessings to each of my clients, check in with my guides, and prepare astrological charts. When I cook dinner, I often make that a ritual too.

We sit down to eat and give thanks for the abundance of food, and our dining room table becomes an altar space—sacred for the task of connecting and nourishing ourselves. At night, I have a bedtime ritual of being in a state of gratitude as I fall asleep.

So, how do you ritualize everyday activities? By understanding the six components of a ritual, you can turn even the most mundane tasks on your to-do list into sacred experiences.

Components of a Ritual

1. Sacred Space
2. Symbols
3. Words
4. Generating Power
5. Gratitude
6. Closing the Circle

Step-by-Step Process to Holding a Ritual

We incorporate these components into our rituals through a step-by-step process. For everyday rituals, you can move through this process in a few minutes by simplifying the steps or using visualization. For more ceremonial rituals, take your time. With each step, you generate magical energy and create a container within which to safely focus that energy.

STEP ONE: SET AN INTENTION

Set the intention for the ritual. Is it a healing ritual? A ritual to honor the ancestors or deities? A working ritual to send energy to a specific intention? A ritual for divination work?

STEP TWO: PREPARE YOUR RITUAL

Prepare your ritual. Assemble your sacred objects and symbols, write your script, and gather any materials you'll be using to make amulets, potions, or food; plus candles, etc. Prep your altar, gathering touchstones, symbols for the four cardinal directions, food, and anything else that feels sacred to you.

Spirit speaks in symbols. So, too, do the Higher and Subconscious Selves. Each item we use in ritual has layers of meaning that communicate more than words alone. Symbols speak to our imaginations, and when we incorporate them into rituals, we activate the right hemispheres of our brains: the more conceptual, imaginative, and mystical side.

Words are also symbols, and they are powerful too. Each word not only has a numerological value giving it a unique frequency, but it also has context that has been passed down through the centuries. When you are writing your ritual or saying the words, speak in the positive. Your words are poetry—you're reciting for the Divine.

Make sure you clear and bless anything you gather for your ritual. How do you do this? You can visualize a glowing aura of light around each item. You can also burn incense around the object as you offer your intention for clearing and blessing. Say:

I bless you and designate you as a sacred object.
I charge you with the function of (fill the blank)_____
for this ritual. You are clear of all distracting or negative energy.

Purify yourself, too, by saying:

My body is a sacred temple filled with divine power, love, and peace.
I clear myself of all distractions, known and unknown. I protect my
being with a globe of light. I am clear, pure, and in service to the Divine.

You may decide to bathe before your ritual. If so, consider adding essential oils, salt, or rose petals to help detoxify your system and raise your vibration. Salt is an excellent way to neutralize energy. Remember, attention is power. You don't want to bring distraction into your ritual; and nothing is more distracting than a lingering negative thought, even if it's only there in the background.

STEP THREE: CAST A CIRCLE

We cast (or open) a circle because when we're working with magic, we bridge the divide between the invisible spiritual realm and the physical, material one. Magic is a powerful energy, and we want to honor it as such. When you cast a circle, you create a kind of "container" within which you are safe from distractions or other energies. You also create a container within which to direct the flow of magical forces. Circles are protective gateways. Within our circle, we choose who or what comes to assist us. Make your invites before you open a circle.

When you cast a circle, stay within that circle and don't break it, primarily out of respect for the magical forces working with you. You wouldn't leave the table in the middle of a conversation at a dinner party, would you? Think of the invisible forces of magic and your divine helpers as special guests at a dinner party. Honor them with your attention and presence.

It is common to cast a circle by invoking and calling in the four cardinal directions: East, South, West, and North.

The **East** represents the element of air, the element of the mind, intellect, and ideas. Symbols for the East include a knife, feather, or wind chimes. Colors include white and pale purple or pink.

The **South** represents the element of fire, the element of passion, creativity, and inspiration. Symbols for the South include a candle or your magic wand. Colors for the South include red, orange, and gold.

The **West** represents the element of water, the element of emotions. Symbols for the West include water or a container that holds liquid, like a cup. Colors for the West include blue, dark purple, teal, or gray.

The **North** represents the element of earth, the element of practical and material matters. It's the element that grounds us in the here and now. Symbols for the North include dirt, a five-pointed star with a circle around it (pentacle), a basket or ceramic dish, or earthy stones, like jasper. Colors for the North include black, brown, and green.

After you've called in the four directions, welcome any spiritual helpers you'd like to assist you. These could be spirit guides, ancestors, loved ones who've crossed over, your divine helper, God, the Goddess, the Holy Spirit, Allah, angels, or anyone else you wish to include.

Put them all together, and these elements form a five-pointed star. Imagine your circle around this five-pointed star. This symbol—a pentagram—is one of protection. Now, you're ready to cast your circle. You can open a circle in whatever ways you feel led. Here are two simple ways I like to cast a circle.

METHOD ONE: DRAW A CIRCLE

With a candle, your finger, your magic wand, or an athame (a sacred knife used in pagan rituals), walk in a circle around your altar space. Start with the East, as that's the direction of the sun's rise. Welcome the spirits of the East, the element of air. Then, move to the South and welcome the spirits of fire, the element of passion, creativity, and inspiration. Move next to the West and welcome the spirits of water, the element of emotions. Welcome the spirits of the North, the element of earth, and the energy of grounding and protection. Finally, stand in the center of the circle and welcome your spiritual helper or spirit team. Once you've reached the same spot at which you started in the East, say something like:

The circle is cast, and this is a sacred space.

I encourage you to be creative with your words. When you're calling in the four directions, you can use whatever words you wish.

If working with the four directions feels forced or inauthentic to you, you could call different angels, divine helpers, guides, or energies. Experiment to see what works best for you.

METHOD TWO: VISUALIZATION

In addition to physically creating one, you can also visualize yourself surrounded by a circle of light. Close your eyes and see a circle being drawn all around you. Visualize that circle being filled with light as it surrounds you. You can imagine different colors swirling in that circle, each representing either the four directions or colors corresponding to your ritual. Once your circle is complete, take a few deep, centering breaths. Then say:

The circle is complete. I am in a sacred place surrounded by loving, helpful energies. I stand in a timeless space between the visible and invisible.

STEP FOUR: STATE YOUR INTENTION

State your intention. What is your heart's desire? What is your intention? I find it helpful to write it down and recite it in a ritual. If I'm making an everyday activity into a ritual, I will state the intention in my mind and then feel it in my heart. Maybe you don't have the exact words for your intention. In that case, you can conjure a vision of your intention or simply feel what it would be like to have your intention manifest.

Feel your intention with your whole heart, and the words will come. You want to feel positive and energized when you declare an intention. For example, let's say you are doing a ritual to attract a romantic partner into your life. Your intention could state:

I allow myself to meet the person my soul already loves and knows as my partner.

Or, more simply:

I welcome my love to come to me now.

You could also feel your intention. What would your heart feel like if you were on a date with your love? Feel it all and center your awareness in your heart chakra.

You could also visualize yourself as being in love. While you may not be able to see the person with whom you'll fall in love, you could see visions of yourself smiling and happy in different vignettes.

When I knew I was ready to be in love, I didn't have a clue who that person would be. One night in meditation, I saw a vision of myself walking up a staircase in what felt like a future home. I saw the marble countertops and every minute detail. I could feel the presence of my spouse and a happy interaction. I didn't know if it was a future vision that hadn't yet manifested or if it was my imagination. I just knew I felt a sense of fulfillment when I saw that vision. I frequently revisited that vision in meditation because it symbolized all that I desired. I didn't need to know who that person would be; I needed only to feel the love and trust that this would manifest for us.

I offer this example as an illustration of how you can visualize an intention that has not come into a tangible form yet. It's best to keep the details of who, what, where, when, and how flexible and open-ended.

That brings me to another point. Remember, when offering intentions, it's a good practice to say, "this or better." That keeps you open for magic to deliver an outcome beyond your wildest dreams.

STEP FIVE: GENERATE ENERGY

Do you remember from Chapter 2 that magic is ecstatic? When we raise energy and emotion to a crescendo, we can direct it as magical power. Here are a few of the ways to generate energy that we have already discussed in previous chapters:

1. Make something (art, an amulet, a candle, or a sigil)
2. Deep meditation
3. Self-hypnosis or trance
4. Sex (in a safe, consensual context)
5. Experience your feelings in a big way
6. Drumming
7. Dancing
8. Chanting
9. Singing
10. Breath

After you generate energy, there are countless ways to direct that magical power. Here are three ways you can try. I encourage you to experiment with your own techniques.

VISUALIZE
Focus that energy into your third-eye chakra. Conjure a vision of your intention. Let the energy beam into that vision from your third-eye chakra.

FEEL IT
If you're not a visual person, you can try the same technique with your heart chakra. Generate energy, and then feel your intention at your heart center. Imagine your energy like a beam of light going from your heart out towards your intention.

MAGIC WAND
If you're more tactile, you can use your magic wand. Direct your magic wand toward a symbol of your intention on your altar. You could also aim your magic wand directly onto the earth. Focus your energy into your hands and see it as a ball of light at the tip of your wand. Then, send it down through the wand onto the symbol of your intention. You could also direct your wand to the earth for manifestation.

STEP SIX: HONOR YOUR DIVINE HELPERS
I always incorporate this step into my ritual practices. Call your divine helpers and ask for their assistance. Give gratitude for their participation. Here are two examples of how to do that:

VISUALIZATION

After you've focused your energy on your intention, visualize it surrounded by a big ball of light. Pass that ball of light to your divine helper. Watch them take it away. Bow your head in gratitude as they do so. If you've planted your intention in the earth with your wand, visualize your divine helper sending their light into the earth or the ocean and watch them bless your intention and the earth as she receives it.

SPOKEN WORDS

After you have generated and focused your magical power, you can say:

I thank you (state their name(s)), my divine helper(s), for purifying my intent and directing the flow of magic in the ways necessary for the fulfillment of my purpose. I release my intention into your hands and trust you will assist me. I align myself with you and give thanks.

STEP SEVEN: CONCLUDE THE RITUAL

Complete any tasks associated with your ritual, and then protect your intention and say an emphatic yes to magic. I like to say something like:

I offer my intention with a pure heart and bind this spell.
No harm should come to others or me.

Finish by saying:
It is done. So it is!

STEP EIGHT: CLOSE THE CIRCLE

Now, it's time to close the circle. As you do, say:

I thank my divine helper(s) and all from the spirit realm who have assisted me today. I thank and release the spirits of the East, South, West, and North. The circle is now closing.

Close the circle in one of these ways:

VISUALIZE

Start at one point in the circle and visualize the light around you dissipating or disappearing as your attention moves around the circle.

DRAW

You can aim your finger, magic wand, or athame around the circle, starting and ending at the same point.

MOVE

Begin in the East and walk in a circle until you come back to your starting point.

When you've finished closing the circle, extinguish all candles and clean your altar.

WORKING WITH RITUALS

Now you're ready to work with rituals! You can create a ritual for almost anything imaginable. In Chapter 12, I'll share some spell and ritual templates with you.

Journal
Prompt

WRITE AN ENTIRE RITUAL TO OFFER YOUR PRIMARY INTENTION.
KEEP THIS AS A TEMPLATE FOR FUTURE RITUALS.

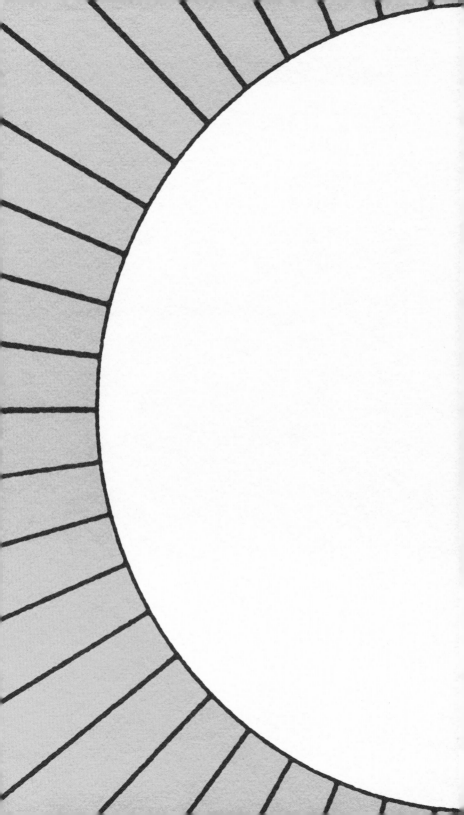

Magic Rule #8 :

Use Magical Astrology

11

When you work with magic, you recognize the complex network of connections and correspondences between us and the rest of creation—plants, animals, minerals, planets, and stars. And knowing even a few basics about astrology will give you a symbolic language to understand those relationships better.

This chapter offers a brief introduction to the relationship between astrology and magic, how to use astrology to time your rituals just right, and how to use it as a tool for self-discovery and spiritual growth.

Daily Practice

Follow the moon through the signs and feel the influence of the astrological aspects throughout the day. Become in tune with the energies of each sign by following the moon. You can find that information on a moon calendar or astrological planner.

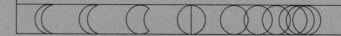

Magical Astrology

Magic and astrology have always gone hand in hand. Both can be gateways to an enriched spiritual experience. Both work with correspondences and see the interrelatedness of all things. When you start to learn astrology, you can't help but contemplate your intrinsic connectedness to the cosmos and all of creation.

When I began to study astrology seriously, I was working as a waitress. I could predict the flow of business by tracking the moon sign, which changes every two and a half days. For example, customers wanted to eat more when the moon was in Taurus and Cancer, but I generally didn't make as much in tips. When the moon was in Gemini, Libra, or Aquarius, the restaurant was busier, and customers were more talkative. At the beginning of my shift, my fellow servers would ask me what to expect for the evening. My predictions were right every time. Through this experiment, I learned to feel each sign's energy, and you can, too!

When you're working with magic, being more in tune with astrology helps you:

1. Have a set of symbols to use when signs and synchronicities happen.

2. Maximize the power of rituals, spells, and other magical activities.

In *The Emerald Tablet of Hermes* Trismegistus writes, "As above, so below, as within, so without, as the universe, so the soul." I have always loved this quote because it helps us see the invisible threads of subtle energies that link us to everything.

AS ABOVE	The firmament: The planets, asteroids, stars, galaxies, black holes, comets, and quasars.
AS BELOW	Earthly creation: From the smallest molecules of matter to the vast oceans and everything between.
AS WITHIN	Your emotions, thoughts, beliefs, and desires.
AS WITHOUT	The emotions, thoughts, beliefs, and desires that exist outside of yourself.
THE UNIVERSE	The entire field of potentiality within which we exist.
THE SOUL	The spiritual essence of yourself.

Astrology studies these relationships and our earthly cycles. Here's how it works. Look around. Almost everything you see—including your hands, legs, and feet—has a planetary ruler or associated astrological sign. For example, did you know Mercury rules squirrels? Saturn rules our bones and teeth. Venus rules cotton, and Mars rules knives. Aquarius rules the Internet, while Pisces rules the movie industry.

We can also draw correspondences between the motion of the heavenly bodies and our emotions, intentions, and life experiences. For example, the moon relates to family, while the sun indicates how we shine in the world.

When you time your rituals using astrology, you are like a surfer catching that perfect wave and riding it to shore. You use the flow of energy to maximize the effectiveness of your magical endeavors.

Basics of Astrology

Here are some simple ways to incorporate astrology into your magical practices:

CAPTURE THE ENERGY	Plan rituals in which your intentions match the signs and planets most pronounced that day.
WORK WITH SYMBOLS	Incorporate symbols on your altar that relate to planets and signs.
FOLLOW THE LUNATION CYCLE	Learn which lunar phase is best for which type of magical activity.
CELEBRATE YOUR SOLAR RETURN	Plan a ritual to maximize the energy of your birthday.
INVOKE A PLANET	Embody the energy of a planet by invoking it to play a larger role in your life.

Capture the Energy

One way to work with astrology in your magical practice is to see what planet or sign most corresponds with your intention. Plan a magical activity for a day when the moon is in that sign or that planet is favored. For example, Venus is the planet of love and relationships. For a love spell, plan a magical activity for a time when Venus is favored. You could have a ritual on Friday, the day associated with Venus, or when the moon is in Libra, the sign Venus rules. For planetary aspects, consult with an ephemeris or astrological planner.

Here's a list of general correspondences:

ROMANTIC LOVE
Day of the Week: Friday
Moon Sign: Leo or Libra
Moon Aspects:
Moon conjunct Venus,
Moon trine Venus,
Moon sextile Venus

FINANCIAL ABUNDANCE
Day of the Week: Friday
Moon Sign: Taurus
or Capricorn
Moon Aspects: Moon
conjunct, sextile, or trine
Venus; Moon conjunct,
sextile, or trine Jupiter

GOOD HEALTH
Day of the Week:
Sunday or Wednesday
Moon Sign: Virgo
Moon Aspects: Moon
conjunct, sextile, or trine
Sun; Moon conjunct,
sextile, or trine Jupiter

FERTILITY
Day of the Week:
Monday
Moon Sign: Cancer
Moon Aspects: Moon
conjunct, sextile, or trine
Sun; Moon conjunct,
sextile, or trine Jupiter;
Moon conjunct, sextile,
or trine Venus

CAREER
Day of the Week:
Thursday, Friday,
or Saturday
Moon Sign: Taurus,
Capricorn, or Aquarius
(for future vision)
Moon Aspects: Moon
conjunct, sextile,
or trine Jupiter

WISDOM/SPIRITUAL GROWTH
Day of the Week:
Wednesday or Thursday
Moon Sign: Sagittarius,
or Pisces
Moon Aspects: Moon
conjunct, sextile, or trine
Jupiter; Moon conjunct,
sextile, or trine Neptune

EMOTIONAL HEALING
Day of the Week:
Sunday, Monday, or
Saturday for clearing/
letting go
Moon Sign: Cancer,
Scorpio, or Pisces
Moon Aspects: Moon
conjunct, sextile,
or trine Neptune

HOME/REAL ESTATE
Day of the Week:
Monday
Moon Sign: Cancer
Moon Aspects: Moon
conjunct, sextile,
or trine Venus or Jupiter

COMMUNICATION OR WRITING PROJECTS
Day of the Week:
Wednesday
Moon Sign: Gemini,
Virgo, or Aquarius
Moon Aspects: Moon
conjunct, sextile,
or trine Mercury

LETTING GO OF SOMETHING OR SOMEONE
Day of the Week:
Saturday
Moon Sign: Virgo,
Capricorn, Scorpio,
or Pisces
Moon Aspects:
Moon sextile or trine
Saturn; Moon sextile
or trine Pluto

FRIENDSHIPS/ COMMUNITY
Day of the Week:
Wednesday or Friday
Moon Sign: Gemini,
Libra, or Aquarius
Moon Aspects: Moon
conjunct, sextile, or trine
Mercury or Venus

Planetary Correspondences

Incorporate crystals and gemstones, herbs, and plants as symbols for the signs and planets that match your intention.

Planets

SUN

Confidence, creativity, passion, life purpose, success, fun, ambition, health, father, authority figures, god, gambling, selling, promotion

Colors: Yellow, gold, orange
Day of the Week: Sunday
Astrological Sign: Leo
Crystals and Gemstones: Yellow topaz, yellow diamond, yellow sapphire, tiger's eye, pyrite, carnelian, citrine, ruby

MOON

Intuition, family, home, children, dreamwork, emotions, fertility, women, mother, water, psychological understanding, healing familial and ancestral patterns, self-nurturing, psychic abilities, pregnancy and childbirth

Colors: White, silver, gray
Day of the Week: Monday
Astrological Sign: Cancer
Crystals and Gemstones: Moonstone, snow quartz, calcite, pearl, mother of pearl, chalcedony

MERCURY

Mental pursuits, contracts, computers, divination, siblings, neighbors, memory, communication, education, teaching, editing, writing, language, social activities, travel (short distances), transportation, spirit communication/mediumship, divination

Colors: Purple, gray, orange, yellow, magenta
Day of the Week: Wednesday
Astrological Sign: Gemini and Virgo
Crystals and Gemstones: Fluorite, green tourmaline, lodestone, blue sapphire

VENUS

Love, friendship, partnership, artistic pursuits, decorating, beauty, shopping, marriage, dancing, poetry, music, design, fashion, socializing, finances, abundance, sensuality, romance, pleasure, fertility

Colors: Green, pink, white, light blue, mauve
Day of the Week: Friday
Astrological Sign: Taurus and Libra
Crystals and Gemstones: Blue tourmaline, rose quartz, jade, kunzite, morganite, kyanite, selenite.

MARS

Winning, managing conflict, sexuality, physical energy, ambition, war, passion, sports and athletic pursuits, assertiveness, courage, cutting and cutting tools (knives), action, hunting, taking charge, strength, masculine energy

Colors: Red, orange
Day of the Week: Tuesday
Astrological Sign: Aries and Scorpio
Crystals and Gemstones: Bloodstone, carnelian, red agate, hematite, red sardonyx, iron oxide

JUPITER

Opportunities, success, philosophy, beliefs, religion, travel (long distance), legal matters, wealth and prosperity, politics, justice, expansion, luck, higher education, leadership, wisdom, spiritual learning and teaching

Colors: Blue and Violet
Day of the Week: Thursday
Astrological Sign: Sagittarius and Pisces
Crystals and Gemstones: Sodalite, obsidian, turquoise

SATURN

Career pursuits, binding and clearing, karma, rules, laws, bones and teeth, structures, ancestors, limitations, authority figures, hard work

Colors: Black, navy, brown, dark gray, dark green
Day of the Week: Saturday
Astrological Sign: Capricorn and Aquarius
Crystals and Gemstones: Garnet, jet, black tourmaline, malachite

URANUS

The future, visions and insights, progress, community and groups, volunteer activities, humanitarian efforts, individuality, technology, social networking online, creativity, rebellion, activism, freedom

Colors: Indigo, light yellow
Astrological Sign: Aquarius
Crystals and Gemstones: Feldspar, garnet, ruby in zoisite

NEPTUNE

Dreams, psychic abilities, imagination, the arts, illusions, hidden things, spirituality, empathy, clairvoyance, mystical abilities, creativity

Colors: Sea green, indigo, purple, teal
Astrological Sign: Pisces
Crystals and Gemstones: Blue lace agate, amethyst, aquamarine

PLUTO

Shared finances, secrets, psychology, death, taxes, inheritance, healing, divination, mass media, occult sciences, power, the afterlife, transformation, letting go, magic

Colors: Black, brown, maroon
Astrological Sign: Scorpio
Crystals and Gemstones: Moldavite

Astrological Signs

ARIES
Symbol: The Ram
Ruled by: Mars
Day of the Week: Tuesday
Themes: Initiating change, new beginnings, courage, taking charge, assertiveness, ambition, conflicts, sex drive, action, anger, passion

Colors: Red
Element: Fire
Chakras: Root, solar plexus
Plants and Herbs: Basil, blackberry, cinnamon, clove, mustard, ginger, paprika, pepper, chilies, garlic, radish, mustard, cilantro (coriander), lemon, snapdragon, hyacinth
Gemstones and Minerals: Bloodstone, carnelian, diamond, red jasper, ruby, garnet, apache tears
Metals: Iron

TAURUS
Symbol: The Bull
Ruled by: Venus
Day of the Week: Friday
Themes: Finances, stability, wealth, possessions, self-worth, sensuality, sexuality, security, design and decor, food, physical pleasure, practical aspects of life

Colors: Light blue, green, pink
Element: Earth
Chakras: Throat, root
Plants and Herbs: Daisy, lily, orchid, tulip, rose, vanilla, cardamom, bergamot, verbena, lilac, mugwort, raspberry, sage, violet, hibiscus, patchouli, catnip, peppermint
Gemstones and Minerals: Chrysoprase, emerald, kunzite, rose quartz, moss agate, selenite, blue tourmaline, turquoise
Metal: Copper

GEMINI
Symbol: Twins
Ruled by: Mercury
Day of the Week: Wednesday
Themes: Communication, ideas, travel (short distances), siblings, local community, information, organization, writing, teaching, learning, wit

Colors: Yellow, orange, white
Element: Air
Chakras: Throat
Plants and Herbs: Bergamot, azalea, tansy, verbena, clover, dill, fennel, lavender, lily, peppermint, anise, valerian, caraway, fenugreek, horehound, myrtle, parsley, geranium, valerian, lemongrass
Gemstones and Minerals: Chrysocolla, fluorite, watermelon tourmaline, jade, alexandrite, clear quartz
Metals: Mercury, quicksilver

CANCER
Symbol: Crab
Ruled by: Moon
Day of the Week: Monday
Themes: Family, home, real estate, fertility, motherhood, mother, intuition, emotional connections, nurturing, psychic and spiritual gifts, security (emotional and financial), ancestors

Colors: White, light blue, silver, gray
Element: Water
Chakras: Sacral, heart
Plants and Herbs: Ginseng, chamomile, daisy, lettuce, jasmine, poppy, lotus, water lily, coconut, wintergreen, seaweed, purslane, clary sage, larkspur
Gemstones and Minerals: Moonstone, calcite, opal, clear quartz, selenite, beryl
Metal: Silver

LEO

Symbol: Lion
Ruled by: The Sun
Day of the Week: Sunday
Themes: Confidence, play, games and speculation, leadership, self-expression, passion, creative expression, loyalty, romance, performance

Colors: Gold, orange, red, yellow
Element: Fire
Chakras: Solar plexus, heart
Plants and Herbs: Daffodil, goldenseal, peony, rosemary, sunflower, cinnamon, nutmeg, saffron, laurel, tarragon, honey, frankincense, heliotrope, poppy, marigold, dahlia,
Gemstones and Minerals: Citrine, amber, carnelian, sunstone, topaz, tiger's eye, yellow diamond
Metal: Gold

VIRGO

Symbol: Virgin
Ruled by: Mercury
Day of the Week: Wednesday
Themes: Letting go and clearing, purification, ritual, organization, analytical mind, disseminating information, order, health, work, routines, alternative healing, service, co-workers, hired help

Colors: Navy blue, dark brown, dark gray, white, black
Element: Earth
Chakras: Throat, sacral
Plants and Herbs: Aster, heather, dill, fennel, lavender, patchouli, skullcap, chamomile, caraway, celery seed, carrots, fenugreek, licorice, mandrake, valerian, morning glory, savory
Gemstones and Minerals: Amazonite, agate, sapphire, turquoise, apatite, peridot, sugilite, aventurine, tourmaline
Metal: Mercury

LIBRA

Symbol: Scales
Ruled by: Venus
Day of the Week: Friday
Themes: Love, relationships, friendship, marriage, business partnerships, beauty, romance, flirtation, justice, legal matters, talent agents, balance, peace

Colors: Pink, green, royal blue
Element: Air
Chakras: Heart
Plants and Herbs: Lilac, rose, strawberry, fig, thyme, raspberry, apple, geranium, almond oil, violet, hibiscus, pink clover, gardenia, jasmine
Gemstones and Minerals: Rose quartz, kunzite, lepidolite, malachite, pink or blue tourmaline, emerald
Metal: Copper

SCORPIO

Symbol: Scorpion
Ruled by: Mars and Pluto
Day of the Week: Tuesday
Themes: Shared finances, inheritance, taxes, death and the afterlife, psychic abilities, power, transformation, desire, healing, psychology, sexuality, rebirth, occult sciences, secrets

Colors: Black, maroon, crimson, red
Element: Water
Chakras: Root, sacral
Plants and Herbs: Basil, chrysanthemum, allspice, foxglove, cumin, ginger, nettle, myrrh, thistle, cilantro (coriander), lady's mantle, dragon's blood, pomegranate seed, black pepper, ivy, eucalyptus
Gemstones and Minerals: Obsidian, snakeskin agate, bloodstone, red garnet, red jasper, labradorite, rhodochrosite, ruby, labradorite
Metals: Iron, steel

SAGITTARIUS
Symbol: Archer
Ruled by: Jupiter
Day of the Week: Thursday
Themes: Philosophy, luck, travel (long distance), religion, spirituality, higher education, knowledge, freedom, truth, faith, optimism, gurus and teachers

Colors: Dark or royal blue
Element: Fire
Chakra: Third eye
Plants and Herbs: Aster, narcissus, Christmas cactus, carnation, St. John's wort, hops, hyssop, holly, cedar, vervain, frankincense, cardamom, nutmeg, reed, dandelion, sage
Gemstones and Minerals: Azurite, brown or yellow jasper, sodalite, black tourmaline, Herkimer diamond, topaz, turquoise, lapis lazuli
Metal: Tin

CAPRICORN
Symbol: Goat
Ruled by: Saturn
Day of the Week: Saturday
Themes: Career, ambition, father, history, discipline, focus, time, commitment, corporations and businesses, striving toward goals, determination, success, rules, structures, practical matters, grounding, boss or supervisor

Colors: Black, brown, dark gray, dark green
Element: Earth
Chakra: Root
Plants and Herbs: Comfrey, rue, thyme, patchouli, hemp, mandrake, nightshade, yew, pine, bayberry, poppy seed, carnation
Gemstones and Minerals: Smoky quartz, onyx, tiger's eye
Metal: Lead

AQUARIUS
Symbol: Water-bearer
Ruled by: Saturn and Uranus
Day of the Week: Saturday
Themes: The future, groups, community, humanitarian interests, social networks, technology, friendships, inventions, freedom, intellect, individuality

Colors: Turquoise, indigo, pale yellow
Element: Air
Chakras: Third eye, crown
Plants and Herbs: Lavender, iris, sage, rosemary, orchid, ginseng, bird of paradise,
Gemstones and Minerals: Amethyst, angelica, aquamarine, fluorite, jade
Metals: Uranium, lead, aluminum

PISCES
Symbol: Two fish
Ruled by: Jupiter and Neptune
Day of the Week: Thursday
Themes: Dreams, psychic abilities, mysticism, spirituality, the arts, endings, emotions, imagination, fantasy, hidden things, intuition, compassion, institutions, addiction, overcoming betrayal or deceit

Colors: Sea green, aqua, teal, indigo
Element: Water
Chakras: Third eye, crown
Plants and Herbs: Wisteria, ylang-ylang, willow, seaweed, sage, lotus, violet,
Gemstones and Minerals: Aquamarine, jade, blue lace agate, mother of pearl, pearl, white coral
Metal: Tin

DAYS OF THE WEEK

Each day of the week has a corresponding planetary ruler. If you want to perform a ritual focusing on themes for a specific planet, time your rituals to correspond with the days of the week associated with each planet.

Sunday = Sun
Monday = Moon
Tuesday = Mars
Wednesday = Mercury
Thursday = Jupiter
Friday = Venus
Saturday = Saturn

Lumination Cycle

NEW MOON: THE MOON IS 0–45° AHEAD OF THE SUN.

Favorable for new beginnings, setting intentions, welcoming career opportunities, planting seeds (especially if the moon is in Cancer, Scorpio, or Pisces). Rituals can be done up to three days after a new moon and will still capture that new moon's energy. Often, rituals performed in the new moon phase take about six months to manifest at the full moon of that time.

CRESCENT MOON: THE MOON IS 45–90° AHEAD OF THE SUN.

Favorable for laying the groundwork for projects or ideas you've had in mind, staying committed, being open to change, business decisions, working with the Divine Feminine.

FIRST QUARTER (WAXING) MOON: THE MOON IS 90–135° AHEAD OF THE SUN.

Favorable for divination and seeing what is hidden, motivation, staying the course, understanding and knowledge, speeding up a magical process.

GIBBOUS MOON: THE MOON IS 135–180° AHEAD OF THE SUN.

Favorable for preparing for a full moon ritual, assessing progress on your intentions from the last new moon, being patient and open to guidance, listening deeply.

FULL MOON: THE MOON IS 180–225° AHEAD OF THE SUN.

A favorable time for all ritual activities. It's good for divination, protection, clearing, healing, and prophetic messages. The full moon is a time when we have more energy available for our ritual practices.
This makes it:

A favourable time to charge your crystals and other magical tools. Place them in the moonlight to soak up the energy.

Make talismans, amulets, healing water, tinctures, art, or anything else to capture the spirit of your intention.

It's best to do a full moon ritual at night when the moon is high in the sky or directly overhead. You might also have more vivid dreams or receive messages in your sleep.

DISSEMINATING AND LAST QUARTER MOON: THE MOON IS 225–315° AHEAD OF THE SUN.

Favorable for clearing, letting go, and detoxing. You can banish bad habits or negative thoughts during this phase of the cycle. It's a good time to declutter or have a physical detox from alcohol, sugar, or other unhealthy substances. The last quarter moon is favorable for healing physical diseases and ailments. It's also conducive to ending entanglements with others in unhealthy relationships.

DARK MOON: THE MOON IS 315–360° AHEAD OF THE SUN.

Favorable for self-care, introspection, and emotional healing. We're pulled inward more during this phase of the lunation cycle. It's not favorable for starting something new, but it's good for clearing, before setting new intentions. Work through addiction, communicate with ancestors, and let go of what no longer serves you.

MOON VOID OF COURSE

Look in your astrological daily planner to see the symbol "v/c." This symbol means the moon is void of course. The moon goes through a sort of aimless period after it applies its last aspect in one sign before entering the next. As soon as it enters a new sign, it's out of its void-of-course period, and you're good to go. This period can last for several minutes, hours, or even days. When the moon's void of course, we feel spacey, less focused, and unclear. There can be delays, or people tend to run late. Avoid doing important things when the moon is void of course, like signing contracts, making major purchases, making big decisions, or starting new projects. In fact, avoid working with magic at this time. It is, though, a good time for meditation, journaling, spending time in nature, chatting with a friend, or relaxing.

(The exception to this rule is when the moon is in Taurus or Cancer.)

Eclipses

When the sun, moon, and earth line up in close proximity to the lunar nodes, we have an eclipse. These are like super-powerful new and full moons, and the energy can be quite intense. Eclipses occur in pairs, about every six months. A lunar eclipse will occur about two weeks after a solar eclipse or vice versa.

Eclipses stir things up in our lives and world events. They catalyze change. So, if you are working with magic during an eclipse, make sure you're ready for big changes! In general, eclipses aren't the best time to manifest new intentions. They're better for revelations, healing, divination, space clearing, or supporting long-term goals. They can help you define your life purpose or help open the way ahead to clear obstacles, sometimes in unexpected ways.

LUNAR ECLIPSE

Occurs with a full moon. Lunar eclipses catalyze change from within. You may receive guiding messages, discover hidden truths, or have profound realizations. Lunar eclipses tend to be more emotionally intense, and they are better for letting go or endings.

SOLAR ECLIPSE

Occurs with a new moon. Solar eclipses can bring sudden life changes. They activate new beginnings. At times, the events are sudden and feel beyond your control.

Solar Return

Each year on your birthday, the sun returns to the same degree at which it was positioned at the time of your birth. We call this your Solar Return, and it is a time when you have full access to the sun's powerful energy. Imagine it shining right on you, asking what you want for your birthday. Your Solar Return is a favorable time for a ritual to invoke the sun's power and supercharge your intentions.

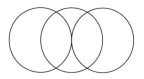

Invoking a Planet

We have all of the planets represented in our astrological charts and you can invoke a planet any time you need to draw on its energy. For example, if you have a big presentation to lead, you might invoke Mercury to help you be a master communicator. If you're involved in a contest, you might solicit the help of Mars to help motivate you to win. Study the planets and learn the different themes for each one.

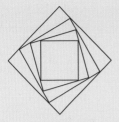

Invoking a Planet Ritual

1. Find a touchstone representing that planet.

2. Place it on your altar, along with other symbols related to that planet.

3. Open the circle.

4. Place your touchstone in your cauldron and cover it with water.

5. Place your hands in the water to charge the stone and receive the energy of that stone. Say:

   I invoke the spirit of (state planet). Shine your light on me, and fill my mind, body, and soul with your warmth, radiance, and power. I embody your energy in ways most aligned to my intention and purpose. And so it is.

6. Take the stone out of the water and dry it off. Keep it with you for at least seven days. Close the circle.

Working
With
Magic

12

In this chapter, we'll discuss practical ways to work with magic in your everyday life. From divination to spells and rituals, we'll talk about all the ways you can harness and focus your magical power. This chapter is very hands-on. So, have your magic tools ready, and let's play!

Daily Practice

Keep a dream journal.

First thing in the morning, write down the dreams you have. Circle any poignant symbols in your dreams. Consult a dream dictionary to see if the meaning relates to anything in your life.

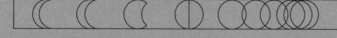

Divination

Divination is a practice that allows your Higher Self and divine helpers to communicate with you. It's a way of accessing your deep wisdom and receiving guidance about the past, present, or the future.

The future is always in flux—changing according to our thoughts, attitudes, and choices. Therefore, divination tools aren't for fortune-telling. Any information about the future is merely a reflection of what will most likely happen if none of the present circumstances change, which means divination is best for deciphering information pertinent to your present-day life, finding meaning in the past, and navigating current decisions.

Traditional divination tools like tarot cards, astrology, runes, or playing cards, work well, but you can make anything in your life a divination tool. My wife and I love discovering new ways to receive guiding messages using everyday objects. When you live a magical life, you don't feel separate from your guidance—it feels accessible at any moment. If I'm in a quandary about something, I will start "psychic" music streaming. I'll set the intention to receive a message, turn on my music streaming service, and pay attention to the lyrics of the first song I hear.

When we were deciding on a name for our baby, my wife bought a floating basketball net for our pool. One day, she had the idea of asking about different names for our daughter and tossing the ball for each one. We both scored baskets for Estella Ray, the name we ultimately chose. Soon, we were using that basketball divination to answer all kinds of questions.

When you start to rely more on your intuition and bridge the gap between your head and heart, you discover that everything in your immediate environment has a message for you.

Here's an example. In my space right now, I'm aware of:

1.   The sound of a leaf blower in my neighbor's yard
        What could it mean? It's fall, and the leaves are falling. It's a time of transition.

2.   The smell of coffee
        What could it mean? The scent wakes me up and makes me alert. I need to energize myself and awaken in order to move more gracefully through this upcoming period of transition and change.

3.   Cleaning spray on my desk
        What could it mean? Make sure my space is clean and clear in all ways to prepare for this time of transition. Do a little "housekeeping" to have everything ready to go.

When I wrote this, I was in the middle of one of the biggest transitions in my life. I was in the process of becoming a mother. So, each of these messages made sense for me and reflected where I was at that moment in time.

        Now, it's time for you to play along! I'll introduce you to another way to use your immediate environment as a divination tool.

Everyday Divination

1. Look around you. Find three objects that grab your attention.

2. For the first one, answer the question, "What does this object symbolize about my intention" Write down the first impressions that come to you.

3. For the second object, answer the question, "What does this object say about an obstacle to my intention?" Write down your impressions.

4. Thinking of the third object, ask: "What do I need to know about the outcome of my intention?"

5. Now, write: "Am I aligned to manifest my intention?"

6. Look for just one object or person to glean insight from. Write; "What does this tell me about how aligned I am to manifest my intention?" Write down three things.

Dreamwork Divination

Our dream time is valuable for spiritual development because our brain state is relaxed and receptive. We can divine information from our dreams. Before you fall asleep at night:

- Cast a circle around your bed and call your divine helper.
- Ask a specific question or ask for general guidance.
- Set the intention to receive information through your dreams. Then, relax and fall asleep.

Keep a dream journal and write about your dreams first thing in the morning while you're still in that relaxed state of mind.

You can make a dream pillow to facilitate your dreamwork and protect you while you sleep. Use a base of the herb mugwort (note that mugwort can be dangerous for pregnant women and too much for children, who already have vivid dreams), which has magical properties, to help enhance your dream state and intuition. Grind it to a fine powder and place it on a piece of fabric.

Keep an intention in mind throughout the process. Do you want to protect against nightmares? Have a more restful sleep? Have prophetic dreams? Use herbs and botanicals that correspond with your intention, but make sure the scent isn't too strong. When the contents are dry, you can sew the fabric into your pillow.

Talismans

A talisman is an object you make and empower with magic. You can make a talisman out of anything—beads, paper, stones, silver.

When you create a talisman, you charge it by focusing all of your attention and magical power during that object's creation. It then becomes a symbol of your intention.

Talisman Ideas

Think of a symbol for your intention. For example, a symbol for marriage could be wedding bells.

Carve your magical symbol into a stone. Drill a hole in the center (if there's not one already), and thread a chain through to make a necklace. Or etch your symbol into a metal disc and make it into a pin or necklace. You could also wrap your magical symbols into a pocket-sized fabric pouch and carry it with you.

When you first make your talisman, wear or carry it for three days and three nights. After that, you can keep wearing it or just bring it out when you feel inspired.

Amulet

An amulet is like a talisman but serves the purpose of protection. Often, amulets are made from natural and organic materials, like a four-leaf clover or stone. They can also be made from written words or drawings. Consecrate yours with a specific function. For example, if you find a four-leaf clover, you could press that into a safe space in your wallet to protect your money.

Herbal Magic

Here is a short list of common plants and their associated meanings;

APPLE: Love, Venus

AVOCADO: Love, sexuality, beauty

BAMBOO: Protection, luck, granting wishes, divination

BASIL: Love, attraction, clarity, confidence, protection, wealth

BAY: Wisdom, protection, leadership, strength, psychic abilities

BERGAMOT: Clarity

BIRCH: Clearing, cleansing

CARNATION: Protection, healing, strength

CARAWAY: Protection (of property especially), health, intellect

CARDAMOM: Sensuality, love, feminine energy

CATNIP: Love, beauty, happiness

CEDAR: Purification, clairvoyance, clarity, focus, calm, healing

CHAMOMILE: Money, sleep, love, peace, purification, meditation, attracts love when added to a bath

CHESTNUT: Abundance, justice, luck

CINNAMON: Energizes you for success, healing, personal power, psychic abilities, love, sexuality

CLOVE: Money, protection from negative people, clearing spirits from your space, passionate love

CLOVER: Money, luck, love, committed relationships, success

COPAL: Love, purification

CILANTRO (CORIANDER): Love, healing, health

DANDELION: Divination, working with spirits, intuition, telepathy

EUCALYPTUS: Healing, protection from viruses and negative energy

GARDENIA: Love, peace, healing, spirituality

GARLIC: Protection from negative energy, illness, or loss, healing

GERANIUM: Fertility, love, health, protection

GINGER: Money, success, magical power

HEMP: Healing, love, prophetic visions, meditation

HOLLY: Balance, decisions, dreamwork, blessing, luck, protection

IRIS: Wisdom, purification, space clearing

IVY: Protection, healing

JASMINE: Love, money, prophetic visions, dreamwork

JUNIPER: New beginnings, fertility, prosperity, purification, strength

LAUREL: Blessings, courage, leadership, opportunities, wisdom, purification, success

LAVENDER: Love, protection, peace, faithfulness, happiness, purification

LEMONGRASS: Meditation, mental clarity, intuition

LEMON BALM: Success, healing, love

LILAC: Protection, love, beauty

MAPLE: Money, prosperity, healing family matters, creativity

MARIGOLD: Dreams, business success, legal matters

MARJORAM: Protection, love, healing (especially emotional healing)

MINT: Money, luck, travel

MISTLETOE: Protection, fertility, healing

MUGWORT: Protection, healing, intuition, dreamwork, strength, divination, fertility

OAK: Abundance, strength, money, power, fertility, stability

OLIVE TREE: Fertility, family, love, marriage, protection, healing

PALM TREE: Courage, energy, purification, opportunity, fertility, peace

PINE: New beginnings, purification, peace, clearing negativity, strength, abundance, protection

POMEGRANATE: Clarity, fertility, blessings, creativity, love, protection

ROSE: Love, spiritual excellence (it's a very high vibration), divination

ROSEMARY: Focus, memory, love, power, sleep, purification

SAGE: Protection (psychic, physical, and mental), wisdom

THYME: Healing, health, courage, love, purification, psychic abilities

WILLOW: Love, divination, binding, blessings, communication, courage, psychic abilities, intuition

Energy Healing

By directing your magical power, you can facilitate a healing process for the body and emotions.

Tap the palm of your left hand 10 times with your right index finger. Now, tap the palm of your right hand 10 times with your left index finger. Rub your palms together for a few seconds. With palms facing one another, hold your hands about a foot apart. Bring them closer together very slowly, paying attention to the sensations at the center of your palms. You will feel some resistance as they move closer together, and that sensation is the energy field, or aura, around your hands. This exercise wakes up the minor chakras in your palms.

Take three or four deep breaths. As you do, visualize light pouring in from the top of your head—your crown chakra—and filling your face, neck, shoulders, chest, arms, and hands. Visualize the light pooling around your palms. Keep breathing deeply, and notice if your palms feel warm or tingle.

If you have an ache, pain, or illness, hold your hands a couple of inches above that place in your body. Repeat the mantra, "Heal." Breathe deeply into the core of your abdomen and exhale. Breath can facilitate the healing process. Close your eyes, and focus all of your energy, all of your power, into your hands. After a few moments, you will feel a swell of energy and then a release.

If you have a loved one who's going through a rough time or struggling with an illness, you can do a distance healing. Ask for permission or, if they aren't available to give it, talk with their Higher Self and ask. Once you have permission, say their name three times. Visualize them right in front of you. Follow the same protocol that you would if they were there in person, generating energy through your breath, and focusing that energy out through the palms of your hands.

You can also do this with pets, plants, cities, states, countries, the earth, or relationships. When we work with magic, we cross the time-space continuum. We bridge the physical dimension with the spiritual one.

Candle Magic

When you have a specific intention, you can consecrate a candle for a spell or ritual. There are several ways to work with candles. You can etch or draw magical symbols or words onto the candle, drip essential oils, or make your own, adding gemstones, dried plants, or oils to the wax. First, choose a candle in the color that best represents your intention.

WHITE: Purity, truth, sincerity, peace, spirituality, air element
RED: Health, passion, energy, strength, creativity, goals, courage, fire element
LIGHT BLUE: Peace, healing, understanding, patience, spiritual growth
DARK BLUE: Creativity, emotional healing, communication, wisdom, opening your spiritual gifts, intuition, peace, water element
GREEN: Financial success, fertility, luck, love, spiritual growth, heart-opening, hope, healing, earth element
GOLD: Confidence, wealth, playfulness, humor, success, leadership
YELLOW: Confidence, intelligence, opening your mind, creativity, self-promotion, manifestation
BROWN: Grounding, the material realm, focus, earth element
PINK: Romantic love, heart-opening, grace, emotional healing, romance
BLACK: Protection, binding, clearing negativity
ORANGE: Success, achieving goals, life purpose, opening the road, legal matters, movement forward, fire element
PURPLE: Psychic abilities, spiritual growth, magic, leadership, attracting influencers, knowledge, water element
SILVER: Clairvoyance, clairaudience, intuition, spiritual insights, mediumship, prophetic dreams, air element

Next, cleanse and consecrate your candle. You can rub an essential oil like frankincense on the candle. As you do, say something like:

I consecrate this candle and dedicate it as sacred. It is clean and clear of all energy except that which I charge it with today.

Give your candle its job; assign it a purpose. Write your intention or draw your magical symbol on the candle. Throughout your candle ritual, you'll receive guiding messages and clarity about your intention. After the candle has burned, look at the patterns made from the wax. Did it drip into any shapes or symbols? Did it leave burn marks on the glass? See if you can decipher any meaning from those clues.

When you extinguish your candle, use a candle snuffer or wave your hand above the candle. Don't blow it out or pinch it. You wouldn't want to blow your intention away from yourself. You can add candle drippings to a talisman or place them inside a pouch as a reminder of your intention.

MAGICAL EXERCISE:

Automatic Writing

1. Establish your sacred space and cast a circle. Gently tap the crown of your head a few times to open your crown chakra. Breathe deeply, allowing your body to relax. In your mind, say: *I welcome my Higher Self and divine helper to convey messages and information of a caliber higher than I could know or perceive with my current perspective. I invite them to work with me in this automatic writing exercise.*

2. Focus all of your attention on your breath. Close your eyes. Feel your aura expand out to the sides of your body and above your head.

3. Place your pen to paper. In a relaxed state, you will start to hear words in your mind. Write whatever you hear. Soon, the words will flow and won't feel like your own.

4. As you write your eyes might water, you might get the chills or yawn, and you might feel your head pulling to the right or left of your body. These are all indicators that you're tuned in to a higher frequency. If you feel none of these physical indicators, don't worry! You're still doing it right. Each of us experiences spirit differently.

5. When you finish writing, thank your Higher Self and divine helper, and close the circle.

Spells and Rituals

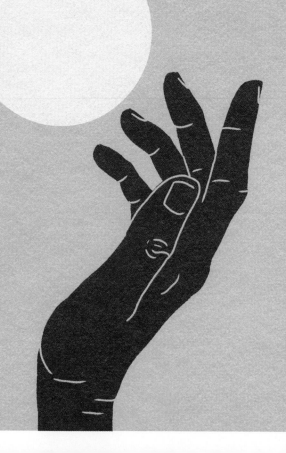

Spells and rituals are ways of focusing our magical energy toward a specific goal or intention. A spell is an incantation spoken while performing symbolic actions. Spells can be done within a ritual or alone. A ritual is a ceremony dedicated to an intention or in honor of a holiday or rite of passage.

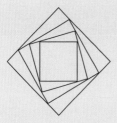

RITUAL:

Divination Ritual

1. Cast a circle and call in your divine helper or spirit guide. Ask your question.

2. Fill the bottom of your cauldron or a shallow bowl with a little water. Let it settle, and then several drops of oil into the water. You can use any oil for this, including olive, almond, or essential oils.

3. Look at the way the oil moves on the water, identifying any shapes that appear and what they mean to you.

SPELL:

Open to Love Spell

1. On a Friday, especially during the new moon phase, make an essential oil or herbal bath tea using lavender, jasmine, and dried rose petals.

2. To make an herbal bath tea break up the flowers and mix them with some pink Himalayan sea salt.

3. Add the mixture to your bath for seven days. While you're soaking in the bathtub, imagine all of your fear dissolving away. Set the intention to open your heart and attract love.

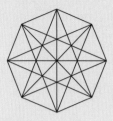

SPELL:

Healing a Broken Heart Spell

1. You'll need a small symbol of the relationship like a piece of jewelry or a gift you received. If you don't have one, you can use a small, clear quartz crystal.

2. In your cauldron, mix purified water with sea salt. Add herbs or essential oils, such as frankincense, myrrh, lemon balm, white rose, lavender, violet, or yarrow.

3. Mix until the salt dissolves, saying: *As I stir my cauldron, I let go of any hopes, dreams, and plans I had for our relationship. I accept the closing of one chapter and welcome the opening of another. I forgive as I know I am forgiven. I reclaim my power and mend my heart. I am whole and open to love. So it is and Blessed Be.*

4. Place the symbol of the past relationship in the mixture. Stir it with your magic wand. Then, bury the object in the ground or throw it away.

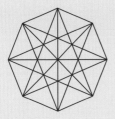

Open to Abundance Spell

1. Make your magical money pouch during the waxing moon when the moon is in Taurus, Virgo, or Capricorn. Fill a small fabric pouch (preferably green) with symbols of wealth and abundance.

2. Add a small coin to the pouch, a green stone like aventurine and any other magical symbols that give you the feeling of abundance.

   Say this incantation:

   I open myself to experiencing great abundance in my life. I am in a positive money flow without resistance. And so it is. Blessed be.

3. Sleep with the pouch under your pillow or carry it with you for several days until you start to see the manifestation of your intention.

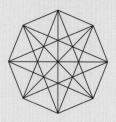

Break Old Soul Contracts

1. You will need a red cord or string. Tie two knots, one on each end. One knot represents yourself and the other represents the other person. Hold one knot in each hand. Identify the relationship dynamics that don't work for you. Say:

   I break all karmic agreements with _____ (say the name of the other individual). I render all contracts from past, present, and future lifetimes null and void. I will maintain the love and positive aspects of the relationship in this lifetime. I will release all unhealthy relationship dynamics. (For example, you might say, I will release any power struggles and push/pull dynamics.)

2. Cut the string between the two knots. Now say:

   The contract has been broken. From this day forward, we create a new agreement based on mutual respect. May it unfold according to our best and highest good. So mote it be.

3. When you finish the spell, discard the cord and knots. You can burn, bury, or throw them away.

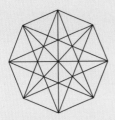

SPELL:

Bind Up Negativity Spell

1. Write down any negative feelings you've had on a piece of paper. Fold the paper tightly and tie it onto a potato with some red string. Say:

   I bind up all negativity being directed towards me from the past, present and future. I am safe from harm. I am protected. I send any negative or unwanted energy into the heart of the Divine for transmutation. So it is.

2. Bury the potato and place a stone on top.

RITUAL:

Fertility Ritual

1. Cast a circle and light a green candle. Fill a small pot with soil. Press the seed of a herb or flower that represents fertility into the filled pot and sprinkle with water.

2. Feel the presence of the Divine Feminine. Open your heart to the possibility of becoming a parent. Offer gratitude for the gift of life. Visualize yourself as a parent.

3. Water the seedling and place it in an environment in which it will thrive. Now you can close the circle.

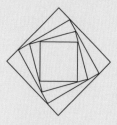

A Space Clearing Ritual

SMOKE CLEARING

1.   Consider the spiritual tradition closest to your ancestry and research what plants and herbs they used for purification and ritual. Tie together your plants with string. Set them on fire and let the flames subside. Purifying smoke will rise.

2.   Start with the front door, and say: *I protect this sacred space. I welcome only loving, supportive, and helpful people and energies into this home.* Move throughout the home, making sure to hit every corner. As you do, say: *I cleanse and clear this space of any distractive, negative, or unloving energies. I consecrate this space as my own, and I designate it as my sanctuary. I clear it of its history, all unhelpful spirits, previous owners and tenants, and painful memories.* When you are finished, say: *And so it is!*

ROOM SPRAY

Follow the same ritual using a room spray. Start with a base of distilled water and add purifying oils, botanicals, and herbs. You can also add small bits of clear quartz crystal.

APPLAUSE

Clapping is another great way to break up stagnant energy.

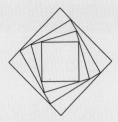

Health and Healing Ritual

1. Mix one part water to two parts salt. Add crystals like lithia or lepidolite for when you're feeling down, rose quartz for times of emotional distress, or black tourmaline when in physical pain. Add the following herbs, depending on your condition:

   ANGER: Catnip, chamomile, lavender, valerian

   ANXIETY: Rosemary, lavender, lemon balm, jasmine

   GRIEF: Honeysuckle, willow, basil, lemon balm, marigold, rose, aloe

   DEPRESSION: Sunflower, chamomile, borage, lavender, dandelion, rose

   STRESS: Echinacea, thyme, lemon balm, aloe, yarrow, catnip, geranium

   FEAR: Ginger, water lily, basil, sage, nettle, cinnamon

   ILLNESS: Ginger, oregano, olive leaf, echinacea, basil, aloe, frankincense, myrrh, pepper

   PHYSICAL PAIN: Rosemary, frankincense, myrrh, rose, aloe, honeysuckle, lemon balm, mugwort, sage

2. Set the mixture in a sunny spot for three days. Then, add it to a ritual bath. As you soak in the bath, say:

   Heal my body, mind, and spirit on all levels. Cleanse my aura and purify my body. I am healthy and free of stress, anger, fear, and all other low-vibrational energies. And so it is.

Living Your Magical Life

LUCKY

13

Now, you're ready to embody your magic—your power. You have eight simple magic rules to follow for working with magic in your everyday life.

1. **Trust Yourself**
2. **Magic Is Power**
3. **Attention Is Power**
4. **Embrace Your Dark Side**
5. **Be Whole**
6. **Relax and Allow**
7. **Ritualize It**
8. **Use Magical Astrology**

Daily Practice

What brings you joy?
Do one joyful thing each day
for at least 20 minutes.

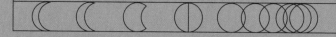

What's Your Mission?

My own Magic Crisis of infertility led me to into a three-year quest to understand our inherent power. It also inspired a sense of purpose—to become one of the voices raised in adulation to anyone who's ever felt powerless in the world. Your light shines. I see you! Your presence is your power.

You will journey through uninspired phases when you don't feel magical at all. You'll feel stuck, depressed, or disconnected from the most sacred parts of yourself. You are no less magical in those times than when you're manifesting the life of your dreams. Remember, magic works in mysterious ways. Those bleak periods could become the most creative and fertile times of your life. I know. In the darkness of my disappointment and doubt, magic planted two seeds that later sprouted in my life—one was this book and the other was our baby, Stella.

When you start experiencing your magical power on a day-to-day basis, you feel exhilarated with possibility. Eventually, your whole worldview changes, and you see how your individual work with magic weaves into the collective magical field. You begin to hear your Divine Self calling you home into the light, but you realize ... that light exists here on earth. You want to be more a part of it; to feel alive in your body and to participate in shaping our shared reality. The more powerful you are, the more you influence the world.

At the same time, you might look at what's happening in the world and think, "Where do I start?" The answer to this question is the same as the answer to "How do I start working with magic?" Start in your everyday life with simple changes that you can easily incorporate into your day. What brings you joy? What inspires enthusiasm? What lights you up from the inside out? Do more of that.

Writing a personal mission statement is a magical act. It tells the universe, your divine helpers, and all aspects of yourself, "This is what I'll do, and this is who I am here to serve. No compromises!" Your mission statement will change as you grow. However, it's a good starting point to help you decide how to work with your magic and contribute to the world.

MAGICAL EXERCISE:

Define Your Mission

1. What is one compliment I often hear about myself? At the end of my life, what is the one common theme my loved ones will say about me? For what do I want to be known? What activities or people energize me the most?

2. Based on these answers, come up with a mission statement for your life, one that defines your values and purpose. Here are some examples:

To be a light-worker, using my gifts of intuition and energy healing to help others realize their potential, heal from the past, and live more purposeful lives.
To bring more beauty into the world through my art.
To improve the world by spreading laughter through comedy.

3. What is your mission statement? Write it and keep refining it until it resonates to the core.

Structuring a Monthly Magical Practice

Magic is part structure and part "woo." It uses your whole brain—both right and left hemispheres, logic and intuition. To become more proficient in our magical practices, we need to weave them into our daily lives in a defined way. Like anything you want to do well, practice makes perfect. Schedules, routines, habits, and daily practices provide a structure within which your spirit can work. At the same time, we don't want to be too rigid. Write down the answers to these questions:

How can I incorporate more joy into my monthly schedule?
Daily? Weekly?
What is one way this year I can build community and share my gifts with others?
What is one thing I can do daily to use my magic?

Look at the answers to those questions as you complete this exercise.

On next month's calendar, add the following to your schedule:

- **EACH DAY**—at least five minutes spent working with magic.

- **EACH WEEK**—at least one hour of an activity that brings you joy. (You can break this up into 20-minute intervals.)

- **EACH MONTH**—at least 45 minutes of connecting with a person who energizes you.

- **EACH MONTH**—at least one day off to relax and "allow".

- **EACH MONTH**—at least one ritual by yourself or with others.

- **BONUS**—add one daily practice from this book to your monthly schedule. Write it in and make it a priority.

Open Your Spiritual Gifts

Now that we have the structure let's add in the "woo". Throughout this book, I've shared ways to develop your spiritual gifts. We've learned to read auras, work with divination, and access intuition. Now, I'll stretch your imagination about what else is possible.

Remember when you were a child playing outside. Did you imagine you could fly? Pretend you were a superhero? Did you wonder whether your backyard contained buried treasure? In childhood, we stand at the threshold between the magical realms and our three-dimensional world. When we play, we can cross from one to another. As we grow, we learn that being an adult means staying on the 3D side. But more of your spiritual gifts lie just beyond the threshold. If you want to open them, you just need to return to a childlike state with a curious mind and heart. And suspend disbelief.

The Lucky Cat

On a trip to Montreal, I wandered into a store in Chinatown. For some magical reason, I felt led to buy a *Maneki-neko*, or "lucky cat." According to Japanese tradition, if you place the cat in your business, it will attract customers. For months, the lucky cat sat on my desk without any motion, and I thought it was broken.

One night, something pulled my attention over to look at the lucky cat. Suddenly, the arm waved—just the one time. I was exhausted from a long workday, and I questioned if I had imagined it. As soon as I had that thought, it waved again. For several minutes, I practiced focusing my attention and directing my energy towards the cat. The arm moved each time. I continued to experiment for several months, with childlike curiosity.

I never imagined it would be possible to move objects with my mind, but this discovery opened me to new possibilities. I have since used this technique to move slow traffic, part clouds for the sun to shine, or free up a parking space in a crowded garage. Here's how ...

Bow and Arrow

1. Imagine your body is a bow.

2. Pull in energy with your breath and imagine that energy like an arrow. Imagine drawing this energy through your back behind your heart.

3. Focus all of your attention on your target. Then, let go. Send the energy flying toward the object. When I say, "Let go," I mean release attention, relax, and trust.

This exercise takes some practice. It helps to start with something simple, like the smoke from incense. It works best if you are confident in your outcome.

Opening your spiritual gifts is like waking up your inner child and inviting them to play. The more you step over that threshold into the imaginative, magical realms, the more you avail yourself of mystical encounters and supernatural phenomena. Then, your beliefs about what's possible will shift, and you'll become even more curious about testing the limits of your power.

Mystical encounters and supernatural phenomena allow us to bear witness to the presence of the Divine here on earth. Moments of beauty and wonder bring us home to our divine nature. So, it's no wonder we're fascinated by them and seek to learn more.

Oneness is our sacred birthright.

Becoming One With All Meditation

1. Cast a circle and burn a purifying incense.

2. Bring your attention to your crown chakra and forehead. Imagine both of those spaces opening wider and wider. Visualize a bright light surrounding your entire head. Rest your chin comfortably on your chest.

3. With eyes closed, look up toward your forehead. Then, with eyes still closed, direct your internal gaze to your right side, as if you were looking at your right ear. Keep your gaze soft and open. Call your divine helper.

4. Visualize a brilliant light at your heart center. See it surround your body, then expand throughout the room. Visualize that light moving beyond your room into your community, through your city, across your country, and over the world. Watch that light moving out into space. Pause, take a few deep breaths, and repeat in your mind, "I am."

5. After 20 minutes, visualize the light coming back into your body. Wiggle your fingers and toes. Then, close the circle and complete your meditation.

6. If you didn't feel at-oneness or bliss, don't worry! Mystical moments can't be forced, but by showing up, continuing to meditate, and being consistent, you will invite divine encounters into your life.

Give Your YES
to the Universe

Magic unites the forces of spirit with the forces of nature. Your body connects your spirit to the material world. Think of your body, then, as one big magic wand.

During magical practices, you might feel physiological sensations that mimic what fear feels like in your body. When we draw in a significant amount of spiritual energy, our bodies respond. For example, your pulse might quicken, you might get teary-eyed, or you might notice that your breath feels lighter or more centered in the upper part of your chest. These things happen when you have a physical response to an energetic shift. When this happens, take deep breaths and repeat in your mind, "I am safe." You will get used to these sensations.

At first, though, you might fear you're losing control, and that's a good thing! Our Ego Self wants nothing more than to belong to this 3D world. So, it will stop at nothing to keep us in our comfort zones. Fear, mental chatter, distraction, and laziness are signs of Ego interference keeping you from expanding your spiritual awareness.

What can you do if you long to experience more of your magic and you keep encountering fear? Give your *yes* to the universe. Open, relax, and allow. Practice makes perfect. Adopt a disciplined approach, and you will organically move beyond the threshold of fear into the magical realm.

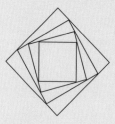

RITUAL:

Beyond the Threshold Ritual

1. In a meditative walk, ask your divine helper to guide you to three natural elements to represent your fear. Bring the symbols to your altar if it is safe and legal to do so.

2. Burn a clearing incense. Create a sacred space and light a white candle. Take the first of the three items and run it through the incense. Say: *I acknowledge the fear that has been with me for so long. I release it into the heart of the Divine, where it will be transmuted into courage.*

3. Repeat with the next item. *I acknowledge the fear that has been with me for so long. I release it into the heart of the Divine, where it will be transmuted into faith.*

4. Do the same for the third item. *I acknowledge the fear that has been with me for so long. I release it into the heart of the divine where it will be transmuted into love.*

5. Write the word *yes* on a blank piece of paper. Raise a cone of power by drumming, dancing, chanting, meditating, etc. Focus all of your attention on the *yes*. Open your palms to the sky and look upward. Say: *I give a full and resounding yes to the forces of magic and the universe. I am willing and open. Work through me to amplify my power so I will be fearless in using my sacred gifts to contribute to shaping a new earth. And so it is. Blessed be.*

6. Run the paper through the incense. Give thanks and then return your objects to the earth.

Living Your
Magical Life

Now that you've dispelled fear and given your yes, you're ready. Consider this your certificate of completion. It's official: you are magical! Congratulations!

Magic isn't to be hoarded or contained. I hope you'll start to share your magic with others as you use your gifts. I hope, too, you will find ways to help spark magic in the hearts of everyone you meet.

As we move through this unprecedented time in history, we are transitioning out of the patriarchal paradigm, but we are still shaping and creating a new one. Although we can see glimpses of what we are moving toward, we are in a shared magical process, which means in the metaphorical dark womb of the Goddess. She wants to liberate us from duality by bringing to light what's been in the shadows. Magic can transform division into unity.

Now, more than ever, we need a return to magic. It is the force that breaks walls, opens hearts, and allows us to be in harmonious relationship with one another and the natural world. Think of what our collective magic can do! Imagine a world dedicated to wonder, curiosity, and connection. By reclaiming your supernatural power, you not only live with more purpose and passion, but you also become a force for change in the world—simply by living your everyday life.

Magic isn't about manifesting the outcome you desired. It's about being open to the unimaginable and impossible—letting your heart sync up with the waves of the cosmos and being carried to a destination you could have never dreamed for yourself.

Index

Magical practices (spells, rituals, activities to try) are in *italics*

Resources

Collins, David J. *The Cambridge History of Magic and Witchcraft in the West.* Cambridge University Press, 2015

Hay, Louise. *You Can Heal Your Life.* Hay House, 1984

Kynes, Sandra. *Llewellyn's Complete Book of Correspondences.* (Llewellyn's Complete Book Series) (p. 4). Llewellyn Worldwide, LTD. 2013

Llewellyn. *Llewellyn's Astrological Pocket Planner*

Llewellyn. *Llewellyn's Daily Planetary Guide*

Llewellyn. *Witches' Datebook*

Lorde, Audre. *Uses of the Erotic: The Erotic as Power.* Out & Out Books, 1978

Melody, A. and Julianne P. Guilbault *Love is in the Earth: A Kaleidoscope of Crystals.* Earth-Love Publishing, 1995

Otto, Bernd-Christian, and Michael Stausberg. *Defining Magic.* Routledge, 2014

Plato. *The Symposium.* Translated by Christopher Gil and Desmond Lee. New York. Penguin Books. 2005

Starhawk. *The Spiral Dance: A Rebirth of the Ancient Religion of the Great Goddess:* 20th Anniversary Edition. HarperOne. Kindle Edition

Caroline Myss for information on archetypes.

For magical tools and ritual supplies:
Magic Hour Ceremonial Teas and Gifts. clubmagichour.com
Mystic Journey Bookstore mysticjourneybookstore.com
House of Intuition houseofintuitionla.com

Find guided meditations and videos of magical exercises at RachelLangAstrologer.com/MDM

Acknowledgements

My heartfelt thanks to all who helped produce this book. First, to Tisha Morris, my wife and book magician, for your encouragement and bountiful love. Much gratitude to my agent Michele Crim for championing this book. To Kate Burkett, Kajal Mistry, and the incredible team at Hardie Grant. You've held the creative vision and brought it to life. To my illustrator Cody Bond and designer Claire Warner. You are all magical.

To Angela Casey, Lauryn Franzoni, and Brett Bevell at the Omega Institute. My writing time at Omega was sacred, and I have you to thank.

To dear friends and first readers Sharon Weil, Robin Keyser, Valerie Madden, Emma Destrubé, Ali Lang, Elizabeth Brunner, and Maryann Russell. Your support and suggestions were guiding lights. To my teachers and mentors. To my magical tribe of friends and beloved family.

To my loved ones in spirit, especially Stella Ray. You showed me what it means to embody magic, and we truly wrote this book together. I feel you alive in everything I love—the owl's song, the starry skies, the ocean waves, and the pages of this book. I love you.

About the Author

Rachel Lang is a Los Angeles-based astrologer, psychic medium, spiritual teacher, artist, writer, and ritual leader with a heart for service. She writes monthly horoscopes for the Omega Institute and LVBX Social, and she's a board member of the National Council for Geocosmic Research (NCGR). You can find her writing and offerings online at RachelLangAstrologer.com.

Published in 2021 by
Hardie Grant Books, an imprint
of Hardie Grant Publishing

Hardie Grant Books (London)
5th & 6th Floors
52–54 Southwark Street
London SE1 1UN

Hardie Grant Books (Melbourne)
Building 1, 658 Church Street
Richmond, Victoria 3121

hardiegrantbooks.com

British Library Cataloguing-in-
Publication Data. A catalogue record
for this book is available from the
British Library.

Modern Day Magic
ISBN: 9781784884611

10 9 8 7 6 5 4 3 2 1

Publisher and Commissioner:
Kajal Mistry
Project Editor: Kate Burkett
Design: Claire Warner Studio
Illustrations: Cody Bond
Copy-editor: Susan Clark
Proofreader: Caroline West
Indexer: Cathy Heath
Production Controller: Sabeena Atchia

Colour reproduction by p2d
Printed and bound in China by
Leo Paper Products Ltd.